.......This page left intentionally blank......

DISCLAIMER

The information given in the book has been prepared by the Author. The Author requests it be acknowledged as the source of this information. The author believe that all information contained in this book is accurate; however, the user should be aware that the recommendations provided in this book do not replace any standard or regulation.

Although the author have made every effort to ensure that the information in this book was correct at press time, the author do not assume and hereby disclaim any liability to any party for any loss, damage, or disruption caused by errors or omissions, whether such errors or omissions result from negligence, accident, or any other cause.

Author
Kamran Ahmad
OSHA, IOSH (M.S)

ABOUT THIS BOOK

This book has been designed for those individuals who aspire to become professional health & safety officers.

The book has been designed by taking care of the point which is to retrieve quick & easy reference to the required material at the day of job interview so as to feel confident of any question that may be put up to the candidate.

Health and safety is of multi-disciplinary nature. It covers topics like biology, physics, chemistry, mathematics, psychology, statistics, social sciences etc. so to cover every aspect of health & safety is a difficult task.

This book covers those topics or industries that are more in demand or relevant in a typical job interview scenario like construction, oil & gas, manufacturing, food safety, road safety etc. It can also fulfill your job's day to day needs regarding health & safety issues.

The material especially photos in this book have been compiled from various public online sources on the web for the sole purpose of giving the reader an impression of what topic he is reading currently. While every effort has been made to ensure the accuracy of the contents, the book is intended only as a training aid and does not intend to approve or disapprove any specific product, service, or practice.

Every effort has been made to give information given been accurate and precise. But in case of errors please notify so as to be excluded in future editions.

.......This page left intentionally blank......

Table of Contents

HEALTH & SAFETY	6
FIRE	11
CONFINED SPACE	15
SCAFFOLDING	18
CRANES	22
EXCAVATION	26
COMPRESSED GAS CYLINDER	29
ACCIDENT, INCIDENT & NEAR MISS	32
FIRST AID	35
FALL PROTECTION	39
S.C.B.A	42
PERSONAL PROTECTIVE EQUIPMENT	43
CHEMICALS	46
ELECTRICITY	50
FOOD SAFETY	54
SAFETY SIGNS	59
WELDING	61
MECHANICAL HAZARDS	63
MANUAL HANDLING	66
OFF-SHORE SAFETY	69
TRANSPORT SAFETY	72
VENTILATION SAFETY	76
TOOLS SAFETY	78

HEALTH & SAFETY

What is Hazard?

Anything that has the POTENTIAL to cause harm is called hazard.

Give some examples of workplace hazards.

- Fire
- Electricity
- Heat
- Work at height
- Dust
- Fumes
- Chemicals
- Stress
- Noise
- Mechanical
- Mercury
- Viruses
- Fungi
- Bacteria
- Hepatitis
- Manual work
- Toxic gases
- Confined space
- Radiation etc.

Hazards in the workplace can be divided into six main groups. Give their names.

1. Mechanical
2. Physical
3. Chemical
4. Biological
5. Environmental
6. Organizational

What is Risk?

Risk is the combination of the likelihood of a hazardous event occurring, and the consequence of the event

Write down formula for Risk.

Risk = Likelihood x Consequence

What is Safety?

Protection against physical harm is called safety.

What is Health?

Absence of Illness/disease is called health.

Can we reduce risk level to ZERO in a workplace?

NO. Risk level can NEVER be ZERO no matter whatever you do to control it. It can be minimized but can never be reduced to zero.

What is safety policy?

A good health & safety policy sets out the organization's general approach and commitment to achieving particular aims and objectives. It provides a framework of general and specific health & safety responsibilities for staff and guidance on the detailed operational arrangements to be taken to protect employees and others from harm as a result of workplace activities.

What are the duties of a safety officer?

- Take risk assessments of the workplace
- Conduct/assist in accident investigations
- Prepare tool box talk
- Prepare monthly statistics
- Prepare the checklist
- Prepare accident reports
- Participate in management meetings
- Arrange the safety classes / induction training
- Arrange monthly safety bulletins
- Inspection of fire extinguisher
- Arrange first aid training classes
- Arrange safety competitions like quiz, slogan poster competitions, exhibitions etc.

What is a toolbox talk?

Toolbox talk is a short meeting that takes place before a task's commencement and may include the following aspects of a task being discussed.
- Job related safety aspects
- Job related hazards/risks
- Control/preventive measures for the task
- Adequacy of P.P.Es and their condition
- What rules / procedures to follow during execution
- Safe work procedures/ methods

What are Control Measures?

These are the measures used to reduce or eliminate the hazards.

Write down types of controls used for controlling hazards in a workplace.

There are three types of control used to control hazards in a workplace.
1. Engineering control
2. Administrative control
3. Personal Protective Equipment (P.P.E)

Write down hierarchy of controls

Hierarchy of controls is as follows:
1. Elimination
2. Substitution
3. Engineering control
4. Administrative control
5. Personal Protective Equipment (P.P.E)

Write down reasons for having health and safety at a workplace.

There are three reasons for having health and safety at a workplace.
1. Moral
2. Legal
3. Financial

What is the purpose of health & safety?

- Physical, Mental and Social Welfare of Workers.
- To reduce the adverse effects due to work on workers.
- To provide workers better place.
- **What is meant by SOP?**
- SOP – Safe Operating Procedure.
- **What is meant by the abbreviation HAZOP?**
- HAZOP – Hazard Operability Study.

Write down types of safety.

Normative safety
- Normative safety is a term used to describe products or designs that meet applicable design standards and protection.

Substantive safety
- Substantive, or objective safety means that the real-world safety history is favorable, whether or not standards are met.

Perceived safety
- Perceived, or subjective safety refers to the level of comfort of users.

What is Method of Statement?

It is the document submitted by contractor to client, covering the general work procedure of a particular job in safe manners as per required standard.

What is JSA and its use?

JSA stands for Job safety analysis. It is the step by step analysis of a job to determine the safe working procedures. A method for formulating a Safe System of Work.

It follows the **SREDIM** principle/steps to be implemented:
- Select the job to be analyzed.
- Record the steps in the process.
- Examine the component parts of the job.
- Develop control measures.
- Install the safe system.
- Maintain and monitor the safe system.

What is safety inspection?

A formal inspection by a team of inspectors who go round an area or section of work to check on standards; e.g. floor condition, warning signs, fire equipment etc.

What is safety survey?

An in-depth examination of specific procedures such as the introduction of new equipment, or investigating a rise in accident or incident rate.

What is color coding system?

This system followed to inspect and insure the serviceability of tools, equipment periodically (normally it is monthly) like fire extinguishers, full body harness, lifting gears, electrical codes and power tools, etc. These things are inspected by competent person and are indicated by putting the color of particular month (this color is decided in advance and is being followed by all people at particular site). The items which are found defective or unserviceable will not be color coded and has to be removed from service.

Who can color code?

A competent person.

Who is a competent person?

A person who has **K.A.T.E**. Which means that the person has required **K**nowledge, **A**bility, **T**raining and **E**xperience for the job to be considered a competent person for it.

What is the importance of a tool-box meeting?

The workers can be educated about safe work rules and procedures, and their awareness can be improved on some task.

What are maintenance inspections?

Inspections involving examining, testing and making repairs/adjustments to such items, often specified by the manufacturer or supplier.

What is a risk assessment?

The formal process of identifying preventive and protective measures by evaluating the risks arising from a hazard, taking into account the adequacy of any existing controls, and deciding whether or not the risk is acceptable.
Risk assessment is a method of estimating the rate of risk of an activity, by classifying actual and potential consequence and finding out mitigation actions to limit that risk.

List the five basic steps involved in Risk Assessment?

- Identify the hazards
- Decide who might be harmed and how
- Evaluate the risks & decide on controls/precautions
- Record your findings and implement them
- Review your assessments and update as necessary.

What is Safe System of Work (SSoW)?

A Safe System of Work (SSoW) is a formal procedure based on a systematic examination of work in order to identify the hazards. It defines safe methods of working that eliminate those hazards, or minimize the risks associated with them.

When a Safe System of Work is required?

A Safe System of Work (SSoW) is needed when hazards cannot be physically eliminated and some element of risk remains. Remember non-routine work as well as normal operations.

What is employee hand book?

Key document laying out company policy and certain procedures, Effective as part of induction training.

List four key elements of Safety Management Systems?

- Policy
- Planning
- Measuring performance
- Reviewing performance
- Implementation and operation
- Auditing.

What two elements should be included in audits of Safety and Health Management systems?

- Formal audits
- Regular and Ad-hoc Inspections.

What is P.E.M.E?

P.E.M.E stands for People, Plant, Equipment, Material, and Environment. A safe system of work combines all these elements In order to be effective.

How do you do Risk Management in a workplace?

Risk Management of workplace is achieved by:
- Identify all the hazards.
- Assess the risks.
- Eliminate or control the risks.
- Monitor and improve the workplace.

Name two types of monitoring methods that can be used to determine whether health and safety objectives are being achieved?

- Active monitoring – checking compliance with health and safety activities.
- Reactive monitoring – investigation and analysis of system failures.

Explain the abbreviation FMEA?

FMEA – Failure Model and Effect Analysis.

What is Permit to Work (PTW)?

An authorizing document approved by management, describing the work to be carried on, identifying the potential hazards or interacting activities that can take place, specifying the requirement, precautions requested to work in safe condition.
It is a written document authorizing a person or a group to perform maintenance, inspections or construction work.
The high risk nature of the work is the key feature that these types of work have in common, which makes them subject to permit control. If the work is not carried out in precisely the right way, then workers & others may be killed.

What is the aim of Permit to Work?

The aim of the permit system is to focus everybody's attention on the high risk nature of the work to ensure that:
- The correct safety procedure are in place before, during and after the work.

- All the people who need to know about the work do actually know about it.

What are the sections of typical Permit to Work?

There are four main sections to a permit-to-work:
- Issue.
- Receipt.
- Clearance/return to service.
- Cancellation.

There may also be a section for Extension.

What legal status does a work permit have?

Work permit is a legal document. When you sign it, you will be held responsible if something goes wrong.

What is the validity period of a Permit to Work?

Validity can be 7 DAYS or 14 SHIFTS MAXIMUM.

What is blanket permit?

A blanket permit is a permit issued on the basis of location where the multiple jobs are to be carried out at safe location.

What is delegated work permit?

Delegated work permit are used for areas requiring light control. For example fabrication, yards – valid – 30 days.

How many type of permits are used?

There are two main types of permit that are used.
- Hot work permit.
- Cold work permit.

Other permits as per job requirement are:
- Confined space entry permit.
- Excavation permit.
- Lifting permit.
- Night work permit.
- Radiography permit.

What is hot work permit?

Any work which involves spark flame temperature is called hot work permit (HWP).

What is cold work permit?

Any work which does not involve production of spark flame, heat and temperature is called cold work permit.

What is vehicles / mobile permit?

The permit is required vehicle/mobile equipment having a diesel or petrol operated engine into the hazardous area.

What are the main risks addressed in a vehicle permit?

- Sparks
- Accidents
- Pollution

What are the control measures addressed in a vehicle permit?

- Fitted spark arrester
- Speed 30 Km/hour
- Proper warning lights
- No over load
- Correct parking
- Pollution check
- 3rd party inspection

What is radioactivity?

Radioactivity is the spontaneous disintegration of atomic nucleus emits ALPHA particles BETA particles or GAMA rays or electromagnetic rays during this process.

What is the unit for measuring the radiations?

Micro sever or Mille Rem.

What are safety measures to be taken while doing radiography?

Ensure a competent person is surveying outside the barricaded areas with surveys meters. The crews are observing and following the safety precautions. The controlled areas is calculated evacuated and barricaded with yellow black warning signs a minimum of 4no.s and red or yellow flash lights.

What is the controlled area?

Any area where the radiations dose is more than 0.75 MREM/h (7.5 Micro sever).

What is a Geiger meter?

It is the instrument used to measure the radiations dose (Radiation Survey Meter).

What is the use of film badge?

This badge is worn by the personnel who are exposed to radiation due their nature of duty and this is processed to calculate the received radiation dose of a person during the period normally 1 month of exposure.

What is decay chart?

Is the chart showing the change in the radioactivity of an Isotope by losing mass by decay in certain period at regular interval of time?

Who is an authorized expose person?

He is one who got formal training in the use of sealed source and X-RAY equipment used in industry radiography.

In what conditions a work permits can be issued for radiography?

The controlled area is calculated, evacuated and barricaded with yellow black tapes, warning signs (a minimum of 4 no.) and red or yellow flash lights.

Give examples of Cold Work Permit.

- Pressure testing of plant and equipment
- Disconnection or opening up of any closed pipeline or vessel
- Chemical cleaning
- Handling of hazardous substances, e.g. Toxic / corrosive chemicals, asbestos, etc.
- Spraying of paint and Brush Painting
- Heavy lifts, e.g. over wellhead

Give examples of Hot Work Permit.

- Electrical welding
- Flame cutting
- On site performance of a non-explosion proof electrical task for example the usage of an Avometer, Megger Tool etc.
- Usage of a non-intrinsically safe tool :(electrical power Drill)
- Grinding

Which Permit is used for Vehicles?

Hot Work Permit

What are complementary permits?

Depending on the nature of the work a complementary permit might be required.
This complementary is not a permit but becomes part of the main permit. Like radiography, excavation, confined space entry etc.

What is Isolation Certificate?

Isolation Certificate combines in one document record of all isolation required for a task to be carried out safely. The control and use of isolation certificate are described in `the permit to work procedure. Are Valid as far as the isolation is implemented without limit of duration.
Certificates are Not Permits. They are added to permit to confirm isolation status of an equipment.

Why Safety Training is required for employees of an organization?

To make the employees familiar with the hazards associated with their work, safety orientation and some other trainings are required. Also special craft training is required before start of work. Safety assessment, risk assessment for potential hazards is essential which covers the general hazards and specific hazards associated to the work being undertaken and the control measures applied to eliminate or minimize the potential of harm to the employees.
Therefore emphasis of accidental loss of resources (Men and Materials) to reduce the direct and indirect costs and loss time delays due to interruptions providing safe and friendly environment for timely completion of projects. Thus imparting training plays an important role in loss control and it is a sound business idea to have safety culture prevailing on the construction sites.

FIRE

What is Fire?

Basically fire is the result of a chemical reaction in which a substance combines with oxygen, destroying its form by the heat generated in the reaction.

What is nature of fire?

Fire is the rapid oxidation of a material in the chemical process of combustion, releasing heat, light, and various reaction products.

What is fire triangle?

In order to start a fire, three things must be present. If any of these is absent, then fire won't start. They are:
Fuel: Any material which can burn like Paper, Rubber, Wood, Oil, Lubricants, Gases, Metals like Phosphorous, Magnesium.
Heat or Ignition temperature: A minimum temperature known as ignition at which the any fuel can ignite. This depends on its flash point.
Oxygen (O_2): which is helping in combustion and is present in the air (21%).

How Fire can be extinguished?

Fire can be extinguished by removing any of the three fire elements like:
- Remove the burning material, the remaining materials will be safe. (Starvation)
- Cut off the Oxygen by blanketing with foam or Fire blanket or any other materials which cannot burn the oxygen will be cut off and fire extinguished. (Smothering)
- Remove or lessen the heat with water or use Carbon Dioxide fire cylinder. (Cooling). Never use Water for Electric Fire as water is good conductor of electricity.

What common type of the fire extinguisher is used for fire?

ABC or Dry Chemical Powder Fire Extinguisher used for Solid, Liquid Gases and Electric Fire.

What are classis of fire and what type of fire extinguishers are used to extinguish them?

Class A: Ordinary combustible materials like for example: wood, paper, cloth, rubber & plastic that don't melt.
Extinguisher- Water, DCP, Foam, CO_2, Halon
Class B: Combustible liquids and gases. For example: gasoline, diesel, oil, grease, oil based paint, tar...
Extinguisher- CO_2, Foam, DCP
Class C: Energized electrical equipment
Extinguisher - DCP, FM 200, Halon, Carbon Dioxide.
Class D: Combustible metals for example: magnesium, potassium, zinc, calcium, titanium
Extinguisher- Metal x-type, Combustible metal type.

What are the type of fire extinguishers commonly used and briefly, explain each one?

Multipurpose Dry Chemical, Carbon Dioxide, Halon, Wet Chemical or Foam, Pressurized Water are the commonly used fire extinguishers.

Multipurpose Dry Chemical: Useful for Class "A", "B", or "C" fires. 2.5-20lb. dry chemical (ammonium phosphate) pressurized to 10.5-18 bar by CO_2 gas (8-25 seconds discharge time). Has pressure gauge to allow visual capacity check. 5-20ft maximum effective range. Extinguish by smothering burning materials.
Smothering – Cut off oxygen / close the ventilation using fire extinguisher.
Starving – End the fuel by removing the material going to burn.

Cooling – Reduce the heat by using water.

Carbon Dioxide: Best on Class "B" or "C" fires 2.5-100lb. of CO_2 gas at 150-200 psi (8-30seconds discharge time). Has NO pressure gauge-capacity verified by weight 3-8 ft. maximum effective range. Extinguishes by smothering burning materials. Effectiveness decreases as temperature of burning material increases.

Halon: Useful for Class "A","B", or "C" fires (smaller sizes ineffective against class "A"). 9-17 lb. Halon 1211 (pressurized liquid) releases as vapor (8-18 seconds discharge time). Has pressure gauge to allow visual capacity check 9-16 ft. maximum effective range. Works best in confined area – ideal for electronics fire due to lack of residue. Extinguishes by smothering burning materials, Fumes toxic if inhaled, Halon is ozone depleting chemical – production halted in Jan '94.

Wet Chemical or Foam: Used for Class "A", "B" fires 1.5gal of stored pressure PRX wet chemical extinguishing agent (40 sec. discharge time) 10-12 ft. maximum effective range. On Class "K" fires, don't use until after fixed extinguishing system has activated, Extinguishes by cooling and forming foam blanket to prevent reigniting.

How fire can spread in a workplace?

Fire can spread in a workplace by four ways.

Conduction: The movement of heat through the material (usually solid)

Convection: The movement of hot gases up through the air (this is the principal cause for the spread of fire)

Radiation: Transfer of heat as invisible waves through the air (the air or gas is not heated but solid or liquid in contact with the heat.

Direct Burning: Combustible material in contact with the naked flame.

What are causes of fire in a workplace?

Fire is started in many ways, the more common are:
- Deliberated?
- Carelessness with lighted matches and cigarettes.
- Smoking in Prohibited areas.
- Loss of control, firing of rubbish.
- Faulty electrical wiring and fitting.
- Incorrect use of electrical circuits and appliances.

What are sources of ignition to cause a start of fire in a workplace?

Following are the possible sources of ignition to start a fire:
- Electrical
- Over heating
- Smoking materials
- Hot work i.e. welding, burning etc.
- Chemical Reactions
- Heating appliances
- Friction
- Static electricity
- Lightning
- Improper Storage
- Lack of Inspection

What is a fire extinguisher?

It is an active fire protection device used to extinguish or control small fires often in emergency situation. A fire extinguisher can save lives and property by putting out small fire or containing it until the fire fighters arrive.

A fire extinguisher may keep a small fire from becoming a big one, but you must not endanger yourself by trying to fight a fire with the wrong insufficient equipment. Keep in mind that portable extinguishers are not designed for fighting large or spreading fires.

Classify fire extinguisher according to agent used in it for extinguishment.

- APW
- DCP
- CO_2
- Foam

How to use a fire extinguisher to put-out a fire?

Remember the word **P.A.S.S.** This is an acronym for:

P: Pull the pin.

A: Aim at the base of the fire.

S: Squeeze the handle.

S: Sweep side by side.

Which fire extinguisher is suitable for a particular class fire?

Fire Extinguisher Chart

Extinguisher		Type of Fire				
Colour	Type	Solids (wood, paper, cloth, etc)	Flammable Liquids	Flammable Gasses	Electrical Equipment	Cooking Oils & Fats
	Water	Yes ✓	No ✗	No ✗	No ✗	No ✗
	Foam	Yes ✓	Yes ✓	No ✗	No ✗	Yes ✓
	Dry Powder	Yes ✓	Yes ✓	Yes ✓	Yes ✓	No ✗
	Carbon Dioxide (CO_2)	No ✗	Yes ✓	No ✗	Yes ✓	Yes ✓

What is the responsibility of Fire Watch?

Fire watch is the person design to identify and eliminate fire hazards, alert and extinguish fire in case of any outbreak of fire and to protect the person and properties from a fire. He is the man to reach first in case of fire by keeping a close watch on such hazardous areas.

Name the two types of smoke detectors?

Two types of smoke detectors are: Optical Detectors & Ionization Detectors.

Name the two types of fire alarm systems?

Two types of fire alarm systems are: Automatic & Manual.

What do dry sprinkler systems contain?

It contains compressed air or nitrogen.

What four actions should you take if you discover a fire?

- Raise the alarm.
- Get every one out.
- Call fire brigade.
- Fight fire if safe to do so.

Explain the term Flash Point of a liquid?

It is the minimum temperature at which the liquid will give off a vapor which forms an explosive mixture with air near its surface

What is meant by the term Ignition Temperature?

It is the minimum temperature under specified conditions at which a substance will ignite in the presence of air without an external spark or flame.

Why CO_2 gas can be dangerous to a CO_2 fire extinguisher operator?

Because any gas without oxygen & normal air is asphyxiate to the human body.

What does Air Pressure Water (APW) type fire extinguisher look like?

They can be categorized by their large silver container. They stand about three feet in height and weigh about 25lbs. (10 kg) when full.

What are the components in an APW fire extinguisher?

Two thirds of the container is filled with water and the remainder is pressurized air.

How a fire is extinguished with APW extinguisher?

Fire is extinguished by cooling the surface of the fuel to remove the HEAT element of the fire triangle.

What types of fires should never be extinguished with an APW fire extinguisher?

Flammable liquid fires and electrical fire should never be extinguished with an APW extinguisher.

A flammable liquid fire could spread and an electrocution cold occur if water is used to extinguish an electrical fire.

Also never use this type on a deep fat fryer fire in a commercial kitchen. An explosion type reaction could result.

What does a CO_2 fire extinguisher look like?

They have a hard horn and NO pressure gauge. They are red and range in size from five to one hindered ponds or larger.

What are the components of CO_2 extinguisher?

They are fitted with CO_2 a non-flammable gas under extreme pressure.

How the fire is extinguished with CO_2 extinguisher?

A CO_2 extinguisher puts out fires by displacing oxygen. It takes away the oxygen from the fire. It has such high pressure that pieces of dry ice will shoot from the horn which has a cooling effect on the fire.

What type of fires should not be extinguished with CO_2 extinguisher?

Fires involving ordinary combustible (paper, cloth, wood, rubber and plastic) because the fire could continue to smolder and then reignite after the dissipation of the CO_2.

Would there be any reason to use a CO_2 over a dry chemical extinguisher for an electrical fire?

Dry chemical extinguisher leave a residue after the fire has been put out. If the fire has started on a delicate electrical equipment such as a computer or TV it might be wise to consider a CO_2 extinguisher because it does not leave a residue. A dry chemical extinguisher will leave a residue that can damage the equipment.

What action to take if a person's clothes catch fire?

Roll them in a blanket or on ground or use a non-asphyxiate fire extinguisher

Should lifts be used as a means of escape in case of fire if they are working?

No - Lifts should never be used as they could fail at any time due to fire causing power failure or fire may enter into lifts system making them chimneys.

What essential information is necessary for someone as regards to escape in the event of fire?

The sound of the fire alarm & the means of escape and route to follow.

Give requirements regarding fire exits?

They should be clearly marked. Open outwards. They should be kept clear. And be always available in a workplace.

If you smell burning and cannot trace the source of the smell, what do you do?

You should sound the fire alarm.

Explain the advantage of light water over an ordinary water extinguisher?

It allows greater penetration of the surface or wetting of the fire area.

Why fire alarm push buttons are normally housed behind glass in push button units?

To protect against unintentional operation.

CONFINED SPACE

What is confined space?

Any space having a limited means of access and egress, when subject to the hazards like deficiency of Oxygen, toxic or flammable gases or substances, dust etc. Or Space heaving a limited entrance or egress but that is large enough to bodily entrance and perform the work. i.e., pits sumps, vessels, boilers, tanks, and Sewers etc.

Give some example of a confined space?

Pipes, Vessels, Tanks, boilers, and Tube areas, Silos, Trenches and excavations deeper than 4 feet, sludge Pits Duct works etc.

What are the hazards in a confined space?

- Oxygen deficiency or enrichment
- Presence of toxic or flammable gases
- Chemical hazards
- Fire hazards
- Fall of materials, fall hazards,
- Electrocution
- Dust, sounds
- Heat or cold
- Caught in between moving equipment etc.

Name one hazardous job in a confined space?

Welding, grinding, chemical, use of gas cutting sets, erection of materials.

What is the oxygen level in a confined space?

The Oxygen level in a confined space is 19.5% to 23.5%.

Which of the following is not a Confined Space?

- Boiler
- Manhole
- Tank
- Small Mechanical Room

Small Mechanical Room

The leading cause of death in confined spaces accidents is

- Asphyxiation
- Burns
- Electrocution
- Falls

Asphyxiation

If you need to enter a space briefly "just to take a quick look," you do not need a permit. (True/False)

False

One of the characteristics of a confined space is that it is not designed for people to work in continuously. (True/False)

True

It is OK for the Attendant to go to the shop for supplies/parts as long as the monitoring results are within acceptable limits. (True/False)

False

If you get a permit for a particular confined space for one day, but don't use it; you can save it for the next time you need to enter that space. (True/False)

False

Atmospheric testing of the confined space must be done at the_____.

- Top
- Middle
- Bottom
- All of the above.

All of the above

When welding in a confined space...

a) EH&S must be notified when permit is requested
b) Pure O$_2$ should be used to ventilate the space

c) All Welding Safety as well as Confined Space Guidelines should be followed
d) A & C only
e) All of the above

A & C only

What control measures are necessary in a confined space?

- Enter with Airline Breathing Apparatus sets
- Use 24v flameproof hand lams
- A hole watch to be kept at manhole
- Keep firefighting equipment nearby
- Gas test to be done for oxygen level
- Provide blowers
- NO smoking in confined space
- Use ropes and harnesses
- Housekeeping considerations before entering
- Use of non-sparking tools if there is any risk of flammable vapors being present

Write detailed arrangements for confined space hazards.

Supervision
- Supervisors should be given responsibility to:
- Ensure that necessary precautions are taken;
- Check safety at each stage
- Possibly remain present while work is carried out

Isolation
- Mechanical & electrical if necessary
- Physical isolation of pipe work
- Physical checks to ensure safety
- Sign isolation points

Ventilation
- Increase amount of openings
- Provide mechanical ventilation
- Never use petrol fueled equipment in confined spaces

The ventilation air should not create an additional hazard:
Recirculation of contaminants
Improper arrangement of the inlet duct
The substitution of anything other than fresh (normal) air (approximately 20.9% oxygen, 78.1% nitrogen, and 1% argon with small amounts of various other gases).

Air Testing
- Check for presence of toxic and flammable vapors
- Check for oxygen levels
- Carried out by competent person using suitable gas detector which is correctly calibrated
- Continuous monitoring may be necessary

Should be done for flammable atmospheres (the byproducts of work procedures can generate flammable or explosive conditions within a confined space like enriched oxygen atmospheres, vaporization of flammable liquids, byproducts of work, chemical reactions, concentrations of combustible dusts etc.

Tools and lighting
- Non-sparking tools and specially protected lighting where flammable or explosive atmospheres are present
- RCDs and low voltage equipment may be necessary to prevent electric shocks

Breathing Apparatus
- Essential if air is not fit to breathe due to gas, fume or vapors, or lack of oxygen
- Never try to sweeten air with oxygen as this increases risk of fire or explosion

Emergency Arrangements
- Contact with emergency services
- Practice drills
- Rescue equipment e.g. Lifelines & harnesses
- Train and instruct all staff in emergency procedures
- Top man to raise alarm in case of emergency
- Trained first aiders on hand
- Firefighting equipment nearby

Communication
- Adequate communication system to allow people inside the space to communicate with people outside the space if necessary
- Adequate communication system to allow people outside the space to summon help immediately if necessary

Permit-to-Work Systems
- Written system
- Ensures all elements of safe system are in place
- Clearly identifies responsibilities
- Should include contractors
- Everyone will need to be trained and instructed

Other Controls
- Cleaning and purging
- Steam cleaning

In what circumstances a confined space work permit can be issued?

If properly ventilated, gas test reading are satisfactory, properly barricaded and warning signs are Posted, trained stand by man is present with log sheet, sufficient lightening and low voltage Electricity (24V-110V), proper means of communication, locked and tagged out if necessary, lifeline man retrieval System if necessary etc.

What is "Entry" into the confined space?

"Entry" is when a person passes through an opening into a permit-required confined space.
Any part of the entrant's body breaks the plane of an opening into the space.

What precaution to take before "Entry" into the confined space?

- Ventilate, eliminate, or control the space's atmospheric hazards
- Blind or disconnect and cap all input lines so that no hazardous materials can enter the space
- Lockout/Tagout
- When entrance covers are removed, guard the opening immediately

How atmospheric testing is done in the confined space?

- Test permit space before entry
- Periodically monitor permit space to determine if entry conditions are maintained
- Test all areas (top, middle, & bottom)
- Observe status of existing hazards and those created during entry operations

What Personal Protective Equipment (PPE) are required for confined space entry?

- Full-body Harness
- Respirator (half-mask, PAPR, Air-line Respirator, etc.)
- Tyvek Suit
- Gloves (Nitrile, Welding, etc.)
- Safety Glasses/Goggles

What equipment are required for confined space entry?

- Testing and monitoring equipment
- Ventilating equipment
- Communications equipment
- Lighting equipment
- Barriers
- Equipment needed for safe entry and exit
- Emergency equipment
- Other equipment for safe entry

Who is confined space attendant?

He is one who is aware of the confined space hazards and knows how to react if anything goes wrong, able to maintain confined space entry log sheet etc.

What are the duties of a confined space attendant?

He is responsible for the safety of entrants, should be present whenever people are working in confined space, maintain update entry log sheet, maintain continuous communication with entrants and monitor conditions in the confined space to ensure a safe working atmosphere, prevent unauthorized personnel, initiate alarm for help if in need evacuate the entrants if conditions are not satisfying or in case of any general evacuation initiated contact rescue personnel if necessary etc.

What are the duties of entry supervisor?

- "Entry supervisor" - person responsible for determining if acceptable entry conditions are present, for authorizing entry, overseeing entry operations, and for terminating entry as required
- An entry supervisor also may serve as an attendant or as an entrant, as long as that person is trained and equipped to do so
- Know the hazards including signs, symptoms, and consequences of exposure
- Verify that the entry permit is complete, all tests have been conducted and all procedures and equipment are in place before allowing entry to begin
- Verify that rescue services are available and that the means for summoning them are operable
- Remove unauthorized individuals who enter or attempt to enter the space

SCAFFOLDING

What is scaffolding?

A temporary structure from which persons can gain access to a place in order to carry out building operation.

A temporary frame usually constructed from steel or aluminum alloy tubes clipped or coupled together to provide a means of access to high-level working areas as well as providing as a safe platform from which to work.

What is the function of scaffolding?

- As a working platform - so that the worker can stand on the platform to do the work easily & safely.
- As a platform for placing material & logistic needed by the workers to carry out their job.
- As a platform and walking passage - scaffolding support the platform that has been used by the worker as their walking path to transport the material & logistic

Who can erect scaffolding?

Certified scaffolder

How to erect scaffolding?

- It should be erected on level/firm ground
- Erected by trained/skilled person
- It is constructed using metals pies & wooden boards
- It should be designed and constructed from good and sound material
- Not to be erected on loose earth
- Clamps should fix
- Proper bracing be provided
- Sole plate is necessary at the base of the vertical pipe (standard)

Who can inspect the components used for erecting a scaffold?

A competent and certified scaffolding supervisor.

What are basic components of scaffolds?

- Base plate
- Sole boards
- Screw jack
- Vertical tubes or bearer also called ledgers
- Horizontal tubes or ledgers also called standards
- Transoms connected across the width
- Top rail - mid rail: should be in between top rail and toe boards
- Toe boards - distance between toe boards to top rail should be 38 to 43 inches.
- Bracings - zigzag bracings, transverse bracings, longitudinal bracings and cross bracing
- Platforms
- Ladder
- Couplers - right angle couplers, right angle double couplers, end to end couplers, adjustable couplers, girder couplers, swivel coupler, putlog coupler
- Diagonal bracings for stability
- Split joint pin & Reveal pin
- Putlog end

What are different types of the scaffolding?

- Putlog scaffold
- Independent scaffold
- Slung Scaffold
- Truss-Out Scaffold
- Suspended Scaffold
- Mobile Tower Scaffold
- Birdcage Scaffold
- Gantries & Tower Scaffolding

How many types of materials are scaffolds made of?

Scaffolds are mainly made of the following materials.
- Tubular steel
- Tubular aluminum alloy
- Timber

What is tag system in scaffolding?

A tag system is put on scaffolding, by a competent person, indicating the present condition whether it can be used and whether fall protection needed or not.
Red tag – Do not use (is being erected or dismantled) - Means scaffolding is unsafe or not able to use (only scaffolder can work).
Yellow tag – Can use with 100% fall protection (is incomplete or cannot be completed) - Use of full body harness is required with double Lanyard.
Green tag – Safe to use (scaffolding is complete).
Note: *Safety Harness can bear weight of 2450kg.*

Who can place a scaffold tag?

Competent person (scaffolding supervisor)

What are the details in a scaffold tag?

Location, Maximum loading capacity (kN/m2 or psf), Date erected and date inspected with foreman's name and signature.

In which condition a scaffold cannot be erected?

Extreme weather (strong wind, rain, ice), ground not stable, safe clearance (minimum 10 feet) can't be maintained with live wire, certified workers and supervisor are not available, permit not available.

What is the minimum overlapping of two adjacent planks in a platform?

Not less than 12 inches

What is a guard rail system?

A barrier consisting of top rail and med rails, toe board and vertical up right erected to prevent men and materials falling from an elevated work area.

What is a toe board?

Barrier secured along the sides and ends of a platform to guard falling of materials, tools, and other objects.

What is the minimum height of a toe-board?

Minimum 4 inches

What is the height of the top-rail from the platform?

38 inches to 45 inches

What are the requirements in placing an access ladder on a scaffold?

Provide access when scaffold platforms are more than 2 feet above or below a point of access.
When using ladders, bottom rung must not be more than 24 inches high. Ladder to be at the correct angle (i.e. Feet out for every 4 feet in height) Ladders are to be tied at both sides not by the rungs. Make sure the ladder extends a safe distance (at least 90 cm) above the landing stage. When the horizontal travel distance exceeds 15 meters provide at least two accesses. If the platform is longer, access shall be provided at every 30 meters. The ladder should be free from damage and should be color coded. All access ladders must be tagged.

In what circumstances fall protection system has to be used?

If the person could fall more than 1.8 meter then a fall protection system should be used.
Example - Any activity at an elevation more than 1.8 meter such as erection, dismantling or maintenance of scaffolding pipes, equipment.

What is the minimum width required for a walk-way?

Minimum width of a walk-way is 18 inches.

What materials can be placed on a scaffold platform?

All types of construction materials that are used for particular construction activity can be kept on scaffolding platform but before keeping the materials & tools required for the work on the platform we must ensure load bearing capacity of the scaffolding platform. The platform shall not be overloaded & be fitted with object protection system like toe board nets etc.

What are the requirements for working on a moving scaffold?

Mobile scaffolding shall be plumb, level & square. It shall be moved only by manually pushing or pulling the base. No men, equipment, or materials shall be on the working platform or elsewhere on the scaffolding while it is in motion. Castors shall be locked at all times except during scaffold movement. The temporary foundation or truck set on uneven ground for scaffold movement shall be level & properly secured. The height of the working platform shall not exceed 4 times of the minimum base dimension, if it exceeds this limit outriggers must be installed. A complete guard rail system must be provided. The scaffolding shall be inspected & tagged before use by a competent person.

When should we inspect scaffold?

Scaffolding shall be inspected and tagged after completing erection. Also before each work period or where they are altered, adjusted to rain or heavy winds. Thereafter the scaffolding shall be examined at least once in every seven days.

What is the angle to fix the Ladder?

The angle of Ladder is 75 degree or ¼.

What is the space between the two ladder Rungs?

The gape or space is 12 inch or 30 cm.

With what color a ladder can be painted?

Aluminum ladders & wooden ladders shall not be painted.

What is a life-line?

Life line is component that consists of a flexible line that connects to an anchorage at one end to hang vertically or that connects to anchorages at both ends to stretch horizontally and which serves as a method to connect component of a personnel fall arrest system to the anchorage.

How can we calculate the safe anchorage of a life-line?

When life is used they shall be fastened to fixed safe points of anchorage capable of supporting 2300 kilos shall be independent, and shall be protected from sharp edges and abrasion. Safe anchorage points may include structural members (minimum 4 inches structural member or 4 inches pipes) but do not include guard rails, vents, other small dia piping system, electrical conduit, outrigger beams or counter weights. It shall be made from 10 mm dia wire ropes. Horizontal lifelines shall be installed at the highest feasible point, preferable above shoulder height. This life lines shall be maintained with unloaded sag at the center no longer than 30 cm (12 inches) for every 10 meters of life line length between attachment points.

What is lock-out/tag-out system?

For servicing or maintenance of live equipment or pipe lines where the unexpected energizing or release of energy could cause of injury, lock and tag are place on the isolating device to avoid uncontrolled operation and give details of the lock-out schedule.

Can trestles be used for scaffolds?

Yes - Provided they are in good condition and suitable for the job.

In relation to scaffolding what are toe-boards for?

To prevent articles falling off the scaffold platform, or persons slipping or rolling out under the guard rail.

If you are stacking materials on a scaffold, what must you first of all establish?

The Safe Working Load of the scaffold.

Name two precautions which must be taken to safe guard workers when working on heights if scaffolding is impossible to use?

1. Use of Safety Nets.
2. Use of Safety Belts.

When a scaffold should be inspected by a qualified person? Give four occasions.

1. On each occasion before being taken into use.
2. After being substantially added to.
3. After exposure to severe weather conditions.
4. After being struck by any equipment.

Can a construction worker remove a section of scaffold if it is in the way of the job?

No - removal of any section of the scaffold may the strength and stability of the entire scaffold. Removal of any section can only be carried out by a competent scaffolder and only under a Permit to work system. To do it under any other circumstances is a criminal offence.

What key ground characteristics should scaffold erectors look for before erecting the scaffold?

They should look out for: basements, drains or patches of soft ground which could give way when loads are placed upon them.

When hiring a Mobile Scaffold from a hire company what four key features should be checked?

It should have:
1. Wheels which can be locked
2. Brakes that work
3. Out riggers for stability
4. An internal fixed ladder for safe access.

What is the minimum acceptable height of a toe board?

6" or 150 mm.

A second, lower, guard-rail is required if the gap between the guard-rail and the top of the toe-board on a scaffold exceeds what distance?

800 mm (32").

Apart from a toe-board and a hand rail what other part of a scaffold will prevent serious accidents from falls?

The use of a mid-rail.

List few safety precautions when scaffolds are used in a workplace

- Standard must be on the same level and vertically straight on the base plate.
- The supporting platform wood must be supported properly.
- Working platform must been equipped with safety elements such as hand rail.
- Scaffold must be inspected at certain times.
- Use safety tools such as safety boots, safety helmet etc. when using platform.
- Supervision of scaffold erection & progress / safety reports are undertaken by a suitable experience & qualified person that normally occurs:
    - Within the preceding 7 days
    - After adverse weather conditions that may have affected the scaffold's strength or stability
    - Whenever alterations / additions are made to the scaffold
- The report made after inspection must consist of:
    - Location & description of scaffold
    - Date of inspection
    - Result of inspection - stating the condition of scaffold
    - Signature & office of the person making the inspection

Badly assembled & neglected scaffold have been a significant contributory factor to the high accident rate associated with the construction industry.

What is rolling scaffolding?

Rolling scaffolding is a similar type of construct to support scaffolding but rather than offering a stable base it uses castor type wheels that enabler the base to be moved. This is a useful form of scaffolding when you need to complete work over a longer distance than a single scaffolding construction would permit.

CRANES

What are the main hazards during crane operations?

- Electrocution
- Crane assembly/disassembly
- Crane upset/overturn
- Rigging failure
- Overloading
- Struck by moving load
- Man lifts
- Struck by counterweight
- Two-blocking & Hoist limitations etc.

The main cause for fatalities in crane operations is?

Electrocution (upto 45%).

What are the main types of cranes?

Industrial cranes
- Overhead
- Gantry
- Jib

Construction cranes
- Mobile
- Tower
- Derricks

How to calculate stress on a sling leg? Write formula for sling angle.

Formula: $\dfrac{\text{Load}}{\text{Legs}} \times \dfrac{1}{\text{Sin (angle)}}$

For example for a two-legged sling, 2000 lb. load and 60 degree, stress = 1155 lbs. on the sling leg.

$$\dfrac{2000 \text{ lbs}}{2 \text{ legs}} \times \dfrac{1}{\sin 60} = \dfrac{1155 \text{ lbs}}{\text{leg}}$$

Briefly explain industrial crane types.

Overhead Cranes
- Common in industrial facilities
- Supported by overhead rails
- Components
  - Bridge
  - Trolley
  - Hoist
- Often pendant or remote operated
- Easy to use, little training required, no stability problems

Gantry cranes
Similar to overhead cranes, but supported by a mobile frame which travels on the ground
- Small (1,000 – 10,000 pound capacity) gantry crane
- Large (600 ton capacity) gantry crane

Jib cranes
- Pivot mounted boom with trolley and hoist

Briefly explain construction crane types.

Tower cranes
- Variable height "climbing cranes"
- Used for building construction

Mobile cranes
- Crawler cranes
- Truck cranes
- Hydraulic cranes
  - Boom telescopes
  - May have jib
- Equipped with outriggers for stability

Derricks
- Boom angle changes to adjust horizontal distance
- Often used in shipyards, building construction, oil & gas rig etc.
  - Gin pole
  - Chicago boom
  - Stiff-leg etc.

What are the requirements of a man basket?

It should be designed and fabricated according to standards have party certificates two guide ropes damage free lifting gears the load bearing capacity should be written on man basket shackles with cotter pin only to be used.

Whenever any sling is used, what practices shall be observed?

- Slings that are damaged/defective shall not be used.
- Slings shall not be shortened with knots or bolts or other makeshift devices
- Sling legs shall not be kinked.
- Slings shall not be loaded in excess of their rated capacity.
- Slings used in a basket hitch shall have the load balanced to prevent slippage.
- Slings shall be securely attached to the load.
- Slings shall be padded or protected from the sharp edges of their loads.
- Suspended loads shall be kept free of obstructions.
- All employees shall be kept clear of loads about to be lifted and of suspended loads.
- Hands or fingers shall not be placed between the sling and its load while the sling is being tightened around the load.
- Shock loading is prohibited.
- A sling shall not be pulled from under a load when the load is resting on the sling.

How slings are inspected?

All slings must be inspected before every use and periodically it should be inspected thoroughly & shall be rejected if found were one third of the original outside the diameter of outside individual wires serves corrosion distortion linking crushing bird caging broken wires.

How to prevent electrocution during crane operations?

Contact with energized power lines is statistically 45% of accidents. To prevent:
- De-energize overhead lines
- Maintain minimum distance
    - 10 feet distance for 50 kv
    - Over 50 kv, add 4 inches per 10 kv
- Use proximity alarms
    - Warn when energized line is near
    - "No fatalities" in 25 years, according to mfg.
- Warning signs

How to prevent dropped loads, boom collapse & crushing by the counter weight during crane operations?

Dropped loads
- Operating anti-two block device (upper limit switch)
- Proper rigging
- Inspection

Boom collapse
- Inspection
- Stable base
- No overloading
- No horizontal loading

Crushing by the counter weight
- Stay away from the rear of the crane

What are the requirements of a crane lifting?

Crane positions on firm and level ground with wood pads and steel plates. Outriggers are fully extended tires are off the ground. Certified operator and rigger are available safe load indicator is working the check list filled by competent persons.

What is work radius?

It is the maximum distance where a certain activities for lifting or rigging jobs in progress.

The parts of a crane are?

Boom, Slings, Shackle, Flying jib, Anti-two block, Outrigger, Main hoist, Auxiliary hoist, Pulley, Web slings, LMI (Load Movement Indicator).

What is SWL?

Safe Working Load is the maximum load that can apply to the lifting tool, safely

What is lifting plan?

Is the documents prepare for planning a critical lift by calculating and considering all factors which is going to effect the lift and there by selecting the correct tools and cranes and ensure the safe lifting procedure to be followed for the particular lift, which is used for lifting and what the safe factor is, where the load is lifted, where it is fitted, size and SWL of each lifting tool used JSA and load-chart are attached with it.

What is tandem lift?

A lift in which two crane are used for Lifting is called Tandem Lifting.

What are different types of slings used for lifting?
- Wire rope slings
- Synthetic/Nylon Webbings
- Chain Slings

When a sling is considered unsafe for use?
- 10 wire broken in one rope lay randomly distributed.
- 05 wires broken in one strand in one lay.
- 1/3rd of original diameter is scrapping or worn.
- Kink crushing, bird caging, or other damage or distortion of wire rope structure.
- Evidence of heat damage.
- End attachments that are cracked worn or damaged.
- Hooks open more than 15% of normal throat.
- Twisted more than 10 degrees from the plane.

What safety measure are required for SAFE CRANE OPERATION
- Crane is to be positioned on level ground.
- Outriggers fully extended.
- Mats to be used for stability.
- Crane radius of swing should be barricaded and no one to cross under the suspended load.
- Ensure clear of obstructions.
- Load chart available in the cabin.
- Qualified Operator and rigger to rig the loads.
- Only one rigger is authorized to signal the operator.
- Don't lift beyond the rated capacity of the crane.
- Wind speed not more than 20 miles/hr. or 32 km/hr.
- Anti- two block system working.
- Load monitoring indicator operational.
- Telescopic boom free moment.
- Operator's cabin have clear view and not obstructed.

What factors to consider when selecting crane operators?
- Minimum 18 years old
- Physical exam
- Knowledge (training)
  - Estimating load weight
  - Signals
  - Operation
- Skill (demonstration)

What inspection/testing regime be established for safe working of cranes in a workplace?
Inspection
- Frequent
  - Daily, monthly
  - Hooks, rope, crane operation
- Periodic
  - At least annually
  - Complete inspection - wear, damage, deterioration, operation
  - Slings
- Testing
- Records

Define the following terms which are in bold characters.

Balanced – load equally distributed on each side of the point of support.

Bridle sling – A sling composed of multiple legs gathered in a fitting that goes over the lifting hook.

Competent person – selected or assigned by the employer as being qualified to perform a specific job.

Factor of safety – ratio of breaking strength to the force to be applied.

Hitch "Basket" - loading with the sling passed under the load and both ends on the hook or a single master link.

Hitch "Choker" – loading with the sling passed through one eye and suspended by the other.

Hitch "Vertical" – loading with the load suspended vertically on a single part or leg of the sling.

Master link – a steel link or ring used to support all legs of a chain or wire rope sling.

Mousing – lashing between the neck and the tip of a hook to prevent the load coming off.

Rated capacity – the maximum allowable working load.

Rigging – the connecting of a load to a source of power so that it can be lifted and moved safely and predictably.

Safe working load – the maximum allowable working load established by the manufacturer.

Sheave – a wheel with a grooved circumference over which a rope is bent.

Wire rope – consists of many individual wires laid into a number of strands which are in turn, laid around a center core.

How to protect rigging equipment from damage or environment?

- Rigging components are expensive to buy and to replace!
- Use them properly and store them properly!
- Keep wire rope slings lubricated and all rigging stored out of the weather.
- Treat the rigging as though your life depended on it! Because it does if it fails!
- Don't use makeshift rigging or attempt to repair any rigging components.
- Knots tied in rigging reduces the strength by 50% or more!

What are basic sling operations practices?

- Whenever any sling is used, the following practices shall be observed!
- Slings that are damaged or defective shall not be used.
- Slings shall not be shortened with knots or bolts or other makeshift devices.
- Sling legs shall not be kinked.
- Slings shall not be loaded in excess of their rated capacity.
- Slings used in a Basket Hitch shall have the load balanced to prevent slippage.
- Slings shall be securely attached to the load.
- Slings shall be padded or protected from the sharp edges of their loads.
- Suspended loads shall be kept free of obstructions.
- All employees shall be kept clear of loads about to be lifted and of suspended loads.
- Hands or fingers shall not be placed between the sling and its load while the sling is being tightened around the load.
- Shock loading is prohibited.
    - A sling shall not be pulled from under a load when the load is resting on the sling.

INSPECTION

- Each day before being used, the sling and all fastenings and attachments shall be inspected for damage and defects by a competent person designated by the employer. Additional inspections shall be performed during sling use as often as necessary to assure the safety of the operation.

REPLACEMENT

- Severe localized Abrasion or Scraping.
- Ten Randomly Distributed Broken Wires in one Rope Lay, or Five Broken Wires in One Rope Strand in One Rope Lay.
- Evidence of Heat Damage. (Cut with a Torch)
- Kinking, Crushing, Bird caging, or Any Damage Resulting in Distortion of the Rope Structure.
- Damaged, Distorted or Field Welded Hooks.
- Damaged or Worn End Attachments.
- *If In Doubt, Don't Use It!*

What precautions to take in case of synthetic slings use?

- Sling capacity varies from manufacturer to manufacturer, no set standard like wire rope has.
- User must look at Individual Sling Capacity Tag to determine Safe Lifting Capacity of that sling.
- If the Tag is not readable or is missing, *Do-not use it!*
- Inspect sling before each days use, and as often as necessary during the day to assure safety of sling!
- Sharp edges can slice a sling in two without warning as the load is tensioned. Use softeners or padding on corners.

What precautions to take in case of chain slings use?

- Only **Grade 8** or better **ALLOY** Chain can be used for overhead lifting purposes! All chain is not rated the same!
- Chain must have a capacity tag attached to it.
- Chains will withstand more rough handling and abuse, but a chain with the same rated lifting capacity of wire rope will be much larger in diameter and heavier in weight.
- Chains must be inspected daily before use and as often as necessary during use to assure safety.
- *It is the riggers responsibility to do the inspections!*

What is safety factor in a wire rope?

To guard against failure of a wire rope in service, the actual load on the rope should only be a fraction of the breaking strength.

The safety factor includes reduced capacity of the rope below its stated breaking strength due to wear, fatigue, corrosion, abuse, and variations in size and quality.

EXCAVATION

What is excavation?
A man made cut, cavity, trench or depression formed by earth removal.

What is trench?
A narrow excavation, where the depth is greater than width.

What is shoring?
A structure that supports the sides of an excavation and protects against cave-ins.

What is Shield?
A structure able to withstand a cave-in and protect employees.

What is sloping?
A technique that employs a specific angle of incline on the sides of the excavation. The angle varies based on assessment of impacting site factors.

Write down excavation hazards.
- Cave-ins
- Water accumulation
- Fire
- Asphyxiation due to oxygen deficiency
- Toxic fumes / Inhalation of toxic materials
- Falls/Access/Egress
- Moving machinery near the edge of the excavation
- Accidental severing of underground utility lines

What is the greatest hazard in an excavation?
Cave-ins are the greatest risk.

What is shear strength?
The capacity of a material to resist the internal and external forces which slide past each other.

What is cohesion?
The stickiness of the soil; a greater amount of clay than sand.

The standard for gas testing during excavation is?
Test excavations more than 4 feet before an employee enters the excavation for:
- Oxygen deficiency
- High combustible gas concentration
- High levels of other hazardous substances

The standard for ladder/stairway during excavation is?
A stairway, ladder, or ramp must be present in excavations that are 4 or more feet deep, and within 25 feet of the employees.

Who is a competent person in an excavation site?
A person who must have had specific training in and be knowledgeable about:
- Soils classification
- The use of protective systems
- The requirements of the standards

He must be capable of identifying hazards, and authorized to immediately eliminate hazards.

When inspections of excavations should take place?
A competent person must make daily inspections of excavations, areas around them and protective systems:
- Before work starts and as needed,
- After rainstorms, high winds or other occurrence which may increase hazards, and
- When you can reasonably anticipate an employee will be exposed to hazards.

If the competent person finds evidence of a possible cave-in, indications of failure of protective systems, hazardous atmospheres, or other hazardous conditions:
- Exposed employees must be removed from the hazardous area.
- Employees may not return until the necessary precautions have been taken.

What are the requirements for a well-designed protective system during an excavation?
A well-designed protective system includes:

- Correct design of sloping and benching systems.
- Correct design of support systems, shield systems, and other protective systems.

Plus
- Appropriate handling of materials and equipment.

Plus
- Attention to correct installation and removal.

Which equals to:
- Protection of employees at excavations

Whose responsibility is it to select and construct a protective system for employees' protection in an excavations site?

The employer shall select and construct:
- Slopes and configurations of sloping and benching systems.
- Support systems, shield systems, and other protective systems.

Shield - can be permanent or portable. Also known as trench box or trench shield.
Shoring - such as metal hydraulic, mechanical or timber shoring system that supports the sides.
Sloping - form sides of an excavation that are inclined away from the excavation.

What are the factors involved in designing a protective system in an excavation site?

- Soil classification
- Depth of cut
- Water content of soil
- Changes due to weather and climate
- Other operations in the vicinity

What measures will be ensured by an employer before starting work on an excavation?

Before beginning excavation he must ensure to:
- Evaluate soil conditions
- Construct protective systems
- Test for low oxygen, hazardous fumes & toxic gases
- Provide safe in and out access
- Contact utilities
- Determine the safety equipment needed

What is different between a flash back arrestor and a check valve?

A check valve allows flow in one direction only. This prevents oxygen reaching acetylene cylinder and acetylene reaching oxygen cylinder in the event of blockage in the torch or line or pressure variations. But a flash back arrestor prevents reverse flow; stop the flow of flame from reaching the cylinder in the event of a flash back or the temperature exceeds a limit (220 0f.)

What is the maximum distance between two adjacent accesses in a long excavation?

A ladder must be present within 25 feet of employees working in excavation. In open excavation,
- At least every 30m on the perimeter, if less than 1.2m deep.
- At every 7.5m on the perimeter, if more than 1.2m deep.

When is an excavation considered as a confined space?

If depth is more than 1.2m.

How is the soil classified? What is the slope to be given for each type of soil while excavating?

The following is a short explanation of soil classifications. You should check the standard for detailed information regarding classifying soils:

Type A soils
Cohesive soils that have an unconfined compressive strength of 1.5 tsf or greater e.g., clay, salty clay, sandy clay & clay loam.
Type A soils cannot have or be subjected to the following:
- Fissures
- Subjection to vibration from traffic, pile driving or similar conditions
- Been previously disturbed
- Or if it has been subjected to other factors that would change its classification

Type B soils
Cohesive soils that have an unconfined compressive strength greater than 0.5 tsf but less than 1.5tsf e.g., angular gravel, silt, silt loam, sandy loam and previously disrobed soils except those which would be classified as Type C soil.
Also includes soils that meet some of the requirements of Type A soils but is fissured or subject to vibration; or dry rock that is not stable.

Type C soils
Cohesive soils with an unconfined compressive strength of 0.5tsf or less e.g. granular soils including gravel, sand and loamy sand.
Also submerged soil or soil from which water is freely seeping or submerged rock that is not stable.

Stable rock
A natural solid mineral material that can be excavated with vertical sides and will remain intact while exposed.

Maximum allowable slopes
- Stable rock: vertical (90degrees)
- Type A: ¾:1 (53degrees)
- Type B 1:1 (45degreed)
- Type C: 1 ½: 1 (34degrees)
- ½: 1 (63 degrees) slope is allowed for only short term excavations that are 12feet deep.

COMPRESSED GAS CYLINDER

Compressed Gas Cylinders are a hazard in a workplace to work with. How?

Compressed gases present a unique hazard. Depending on the particular gas, there is a potential for simultaneous exposure to both mechanical and chemical hazards. Gases may be:
- Flammable or combustible
- Explosive
- Corrosive
- Poisonous
- Inert
- Or a combination of hazards

Since the gases are contained in heavy, highly pressurized metal containers, the large amount of potential energy resulting from compression of the gas makes the cylinder a potential rocket or fragmentation bomb.

Compressed Gas Cylinder can be classified as?

- Flammable Gasses
- Oxygen and Oxidizing Gases
- Acid and Alkaline Gases
- Highly Toxic Gases
- Cryogenic Liquefied Gases
- Inert Gases

Oxygen and nitrous oxide cylinders must be separated from flammables by minimum of how many feet?

20 feet.

How will you identify contents of a compressed gas cylinder?

- Clearly label all cylinders
- Labels should be durable
- Do not accept cylinders that are not clearly labeled
- Color-coding is not a reliable means of identification - Cylinder colors vary from supplier to supplier
- If cylinder contents cannot be identified: Mark as "Contents Unknown". Contact the manufacturer.

What are the guidelines for transporting compressed gas cylinders?

- A cylinder cart should always be used - Do not roll, drag, or slide cylinders.
- Transport cylinders with valve caps - Do not lift cylinders by the cap.
- Do not transport with the regulator attached.
- Cylinders must be fastened securely in upright position.

What are the guidelines for storing of compressed gas cylinders at a workplace?

- Properly secure at all times - Straps, belts or chains.
- Keep valve caps on unless the cylinder is being used.
- Store in a well ventilated area - Keep away from heat or ignition sources and from electrical circuits.
- Segregate Oxygen cylinders (empty or full) from fuel-gas cylinders and combustible materials - 20 feet minimum distance.
- Store flammable gas cylinders away from oxygen, nitrous oxide cylinders or oxygen charging facilities.
- Segregate full and empty cylinders - Label empty cylinders to prevent confusion. Empty cylinders should be returned to Central Receiving/Vendor.

What are the precautions for the regulator of a compressed gas cylinder?

- Always use the proper regulator for the gas.
- Do not allow oil or grease to come in contact with cylinders or valves.
- Attach the regulator securely before opening valve.
- Open the cylinder valves SLOWLY; stand to the side of regulator when opening valve.
- Do not attempt to repair cylinder valves while a cylinder contains gas pressure.

What are the things NOT to do whilst dealing with compressed gas cylinder in a workplace?

- Never roll a cylinder to move it.
- Never carry a cylinder by the valve.
- Never leave an open cylinder unattended.
- Never leave a cylinder unsecured.
- Never grease or oil the regulator, valve, or fittings of an oxygen cylinder.
- Never refill a cylinder (if not authorized).
- Never use a flame to locate gas leaks.
- Never attempt to mix gasses in a cylinder.

What are the things to always REMEMBER when dealing with compressed gas cylinders?

- Always wear eye protection when working with compressed gases.
- Only use regulators that have both high and low pressure gauges.
- Never refill a cylinder or use a cylinder for storing any other material.
- The greatest hazard to a user of compressed gases is asphyxiation.
- Remember, except for Oxygen and Air, ALL GASES ARE AN ASPHYXIANT.

What are the precautions to be taken while handling and storing compressed cylinders?

- Where cylinders are to be kept for an appreciable length of time should be provided to ensure that they cause no hazard to workers or public in the area.
- Cylinders should be stored in a well ventilated area- preferable in open air but protected from the weather.
- The store should be away from fire risks and source of heat and ignition. Nothing else should be stored in the area.
- The cylinders should be stored upright on a firm level, well drained surface free from hollows and cavities. All long grass, weeds etc. should be removed.
- Cylinders should be secured so as they are prevented from falling over, when in storage or use.
- Cylinders should be segregated within the store according to type and weather full or empty.
- Oxygen and oxidizing gases should be separated flammable gases by 6m or by a fire resistant partition.
- No electrical apparatus should be installed within a cylinder store unless it is constructed to a suitable standard for the hazard.
- No cylinder should be used in a storage area.
- Appropriate warning signs "HIGHLY FLAMMABLE", NO SMOKING", "FULL/EMPTY" etc. should be displayed.
- Suitable firefighting apparatus should be situated adjacent to the store. Typically dry powder fire extinguishers. These should be inspected and maintained at intervals not exceeding 1 year.
- Where cylinders area required to be stored in a compound this should be located not less than 3 meters from any building, site or public access road. The compound fence should be a minimum of 2 meters high, and it should have two means of escape, with the gates opening outwards.
- Where it is necessary to take precautions vandalism or theft, suitable protection cages should be used.
- Each cylinder should be adequate marked to include the manufacturer's mark and serial number, together with an indication of the specification to which the cylinder is constructed and its years of manufacture. A date of test and pressure test, together with weight of cylinder and the name of the product, should be displayed.
- When gas cylinders are to be transported they should be protected from physical damage and the consequences of any leaks that may occur minimized
- Move cylinders by hand in proper cylinder trolleys where the cylinder is secured in the trolley.
- Take great care when lifting cylinders as they can be very heavy and awkward to handle.
- Before moving any cylinders remove all attached equipment including regulators and safety cap must be provided.
- The cylinders should be properly supported and secures within the vehicle so they cannot move during the journey. They should be totally within the vehicle and protected from impact.
- The cylinders should be checked to ensure that the valves are closed and there are no leaks.
- The vehicle should be equipped with a suitable fire extinguisher. Typically dry powder, minimum capacity 2kg.
- There should be no smoking within the vehicle while crying cylinders.
- The driver of the vehicle should be conversant with the load and have written information on the hazards and the action to be taken should any problems occur. The driver should also have training in the operation of the fire extinguisher and any other safety equipment carried.

What four essential precautions are necessary when handling or storing oxygen cylinders?

- Store upright.
- Keep oil away from valve.
- Do not expose to heat.
- Do not drop.

- **Which if any of the following substances are normally refrigerated to store as Liquefied Gases?**
- Ethylene Oxide.
- Isobutane.
- Ethane.
- Oxygen.

Ethane & Oxygen

What emergency steps should you take if an acetylene cylinder becomes hot due to a flashback or accidental heating?

- Shut the valve if possible.
- Detach the regulator or other fittings.
- Take cylinder out of doors and immerse in water or drench with water until cylinder is cool.
- Contact the supplier for further advice.

What is the correct procedure for joining a gas hose to a cylinder regulator?

The hose should be connected to an approved hose connector, and all hose/connector joints should be completed by the fitting of hose clips of the jubilee or other approved type to ensure a gas tight joint.

Name one correct way to test for a gas leak?

- By brushing with soapy water over suspected point of leak.
- Use an appropriate sensitive gas detector.

Is it acceptable to store all gas cylinders in the one store?

No - Cylinders containing flammable or explosive gases should never be stored in the same store as oxygen.

Is oxygen an inflammable gas?

No - But it vigorously supports combustion.

What is the main constituent of Natural Gas?

Methane.

What do the letters L.P.G. marked on a cylinder stand for?

Liquefied Petroleum Gas.

How is (a) Carbon Monoxide formed and (b) what is it?

(a) Carbon monoxide is created by the incomplete combustion of any carbon-based fuel.
(b) It is a toxic, colorless, odorless, tasteless and nonirritant gas that is slightly less dense than air and is very soluble in water.

What four safety precautions should be taken to control carbon monoxide exposure in a workplace?

1. Keep rooms properly ventilated when gas appliances are operating.
2. Keep gas appliances properly maintained and serviced at regular intervals.
3. Portable petrol/diesel engines should never be run indoors in a confined space.
4. Where forklift trucks or similar are used indoors in warehouses, etc. advice should be sought from the regulatory authorities or suppliers.

What two sectors or occupations are most likely to be affected by fatal carbon monoxide poisoning?

The occupations most affected in terms of fatal accidents are:-
1. Security workers and night watchmen.
2. Those working in poorly ventilated atmospheres where gas is used for heating.

ACCIDENT, INCIDENT & NEAR MISS

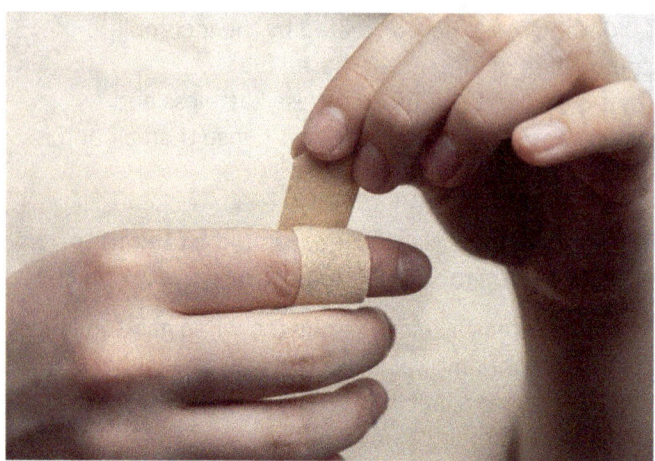

What is an Accident?

An un-planned, unwanted event which result in loss of some kind is called Accident.

Undesired events giving rise to death, ill, serious health problem, injury, property damage, or other loss.

What is an Incident?

An unplanned event that could have caused loss of some kind.

Event that give raise to an accident or had the potential to lead to an accident.

What is Near Miss?

An event which has occurred but has not caused any injury or substantial property loss is a near miss.

Event that had the potential to lead to an accident.

What are the causes of Near Miss, Incident and Accident?

There are two main causes of Near Miss, Incident and Accident.
- UNSAFE ACT.
- UNSAFE CONDITION.

Give some examples of UNSAFE ACT

- Failure to warn.
- Operating at improper speed.
- Removing safety devices.
- Using defective equipment.
- Failure to properly use of PPE's.
- Improper placement.
- Horse play.
- Failure to secure.
- Making safety devices inoperable.
- Using defective safety devices.
- Using equipment improperly.
- Improper loading.
- Improper lifting
- Operating equipment without authority.

Give some examples of UNSAFE CONDITION

- Inadequate guards or barriers.
- Inadequate warning system.
- Poor housekeeping.
- Noise exposures.
- Inadequate ventilation.
- Inadequate or improper protective equipment.
- Congestion or restricted action.
- Fire and explosion hazards.
- Hazardous environment condition.
- Inadequate or excess illumination.
- Defective tools, equipment or materials.
- Access not clear.
- Area not cordon off.

Give some examples of NEAR MISS

- Operating heavy equipment too close to each other almost colliding due to operating activities are close in proximity.
- Equipment not tied down properly on the truck bed, equipment is loose or it falls off without striking anything or anyone.
- Waterblast operators blasting too close to each other without striking each other, but could potentially have.
- Backing up in a forklift without looking back and another employee passes behind without the operator aware.
- Not cleaning up a spill and someone else finding it and cleaning it up.
- A truck arrives to be unloaded, during travel the load has shifted, when the door is opened a drum falls out just missing an employee.
- Kicking a brace and almost falling.
- Climbing out of Bob Cat and foot slipped on step.
- Slightly damaged van, pulling trailer out of dock.
- Sprayed with solvent after opening 55 gallon drum.
- Pallet broke, spilling chemicals, weather deterioration to pallet.
- Sprayed with etch after pressure build-up in line.
- Pressure in a tank caused material to shoot out probe inlet.

- Stepped into open sump when unloading oil tanker.
- Chemical splash, after pressure build-up at filter basket.
- Guard rail broke when employee was climbing down. While excavating an area, a gas line was struck and broken, releasing natural gas. The owner assured us prior to work that all lines were blocked and/or locked.
- An employee reached into a piece of moving equipment without shutting it down to dislodge a jam, no injury or equipment damage occurred….This time. (Shut down equipment and lockout/tagout).
- A major release of flammable gas that forms a vapor cloud but does not explode.

What is Lost Time Injury (LTI)?

Any accident that results in an injury at work that causes absence of the worker from duty for more than one shift/24 hours.

What Is Restricted Work Injury (RWI)?

Any accident that result in any injury whose severity is such that through the worker returns to duty but is able to do only lighter work or other than his normal duty.

What is Medical Treatment Case (MTC)?

Any injury at work place other than LTI and RWI that requires professional medical care by a Registered Medical Practitioner/Doctor.

What is First Aid Case (FAC)?

Any injury that is manageable by first aid or through paramedical staff.

When do you conduct an investigation?

- All incidents, whether a near miss or an actual injury-related event, should be investigated.
- Near miss reporting and investigation allow you to identify and control hazards before they cause a more serious incident.
- Accident/incident investigations are a tool for uncovering hazards that either were missed earlier or have managed to slip out of the controls planned for them.
- It is useful only when done with the aim of discovering every contributing factor to the accident/incident to "foolproof" the condition and/or activity and prevent future occurrences. In other words, your objective is to identify root causes, not to primarily set blame.

Who should investigate an accident/incident investigation?

The usual investigator for all incidents is the supervisor in charge of the involved area and/or activity. Accident investigations represent a good way to involve employees in safety and health. Employee involvement will not only give you additional expertise and insight, but in the eyes of the workers, will lend credibility to the results. Employee involvement also benefits the involved employees by educating them on potential hazards, and the experience usually makes them believers in the importance of safety, thus strengthening the safety culture of the organization. The safety department or the person in charge of safety and health should participate in the investigation or review the investigative findings and recommendations. Many companies use a team or a subcommittee or the joint employee-management committee to investigate incidents involving serious injury or extensive property damage.

The investigative report should answer which six questions?

Six key questions should be answered:
- Who, what, when, where, why, and how.
- Fact should be distinguished from opinion, and both should be presented carefully and clearly.
- The report should include thorough interviews with everyone with any knowledge of the incident.
- A good investigation is likely to reveal several contributing factors, and it probably will recommend several preventive actions.

What are the typical contents of accident report?

- Date and time accident happened
- What activity/task was carried out at that time
- What happened
- Persons involved
- What went wrong
- Causes of the incident (immediate, underlying & root causes)
- Corrective action suggested
- Signatures of safety officer safety, safety in-charge, project manager etc.

Who makes an accident investigation report?

A team of frontline supervisor, HSE manager, sub-contractor, representatives if subcontractor personnel are injured, high officials depending upon the severity of accident.

What is the use of accident report?

To find out the root cause of accident, make recommendations to prevent re-occurrence and evaluate the effectiveness of emergency response.

What should you do if you receive any injury?

You report to the first aid department.

Why investigate an incident even if no accident occurred?

To prevent the recurrence of a situation where somebody may be injured.

Why keep a record of all accidents, however small?

- Accident Prevention.
- In case of litigation.

What responsibility has an employee to avoid accidents?

He must work safely and use all the protective equipment provided for him.

What are the causes of accident of working at height?

- Lack of knowledge and skill
- Over work
- Feeling of dizziness
- Non usage of PPEs like safety belt
- Unsafe platform (not covered having floor openings)
- Improper erecting etc.
- Not following rules and regulations

Name four areas into which accident costs may be classified?

- Wage Losses.
- Production Losses.
- Medical Costs.
- Property Damage.
- Investigation Costs.
- Insurance Costs.

What are the causes of industrial accidents?

- Inadequate skills, improper supervision etc.
- Rapid industrialization
- Expansion of existing factories
- Setting up new industries involving hazards not know earlier

Give four consequences of an accident?

- Pain and Suffering.
- Loss of work and wages.
- Loss of production.
- Damage to plant.
- Nonproductive losses.

What are the immediate and ultimate objectives of an accident investigation? Qualify your answer.

- The Immediate Objective - is to get accurate information about the cause and circumstances of the accident.
- The Ultimate Objective - is to prevent future reoccurrence's of similar accidents, to uncover new hazards, and to devise methods to control these hazards.

When a fatal accident has occurred in a factory, what are the three conditions necessary for allowing the place of fatality to be disturbed?

- The expiration of three clear days after notification to the authority.
- The place has been visited and inspected by an inspector or with the consent of an inspector
- The disturbance was necessary for securing the safety of persons.

Who should have the prime responsibility of investigating an accident, and who should not investigate an accident?

- The Safety Officer, who is trained and equipped for accident investigation. If possible he/she should be accompanied by a member of the safety consultation mechanism, or Safety Representative.
- The manager/supervisor/foreperson of the area where the accident happened. They may be involved emotionally or by sense of guilt.

Is it necessary to report the collapse of a building even if nobody is injured?

Yes. A report must be made to The Health and Safety Authority.

If a member of the public is injured in a supermarket as a result of the work activity there and has to receive medical treatment, is the accident reportable to the Health and Safety Authority?

Yes.

FIRST AID

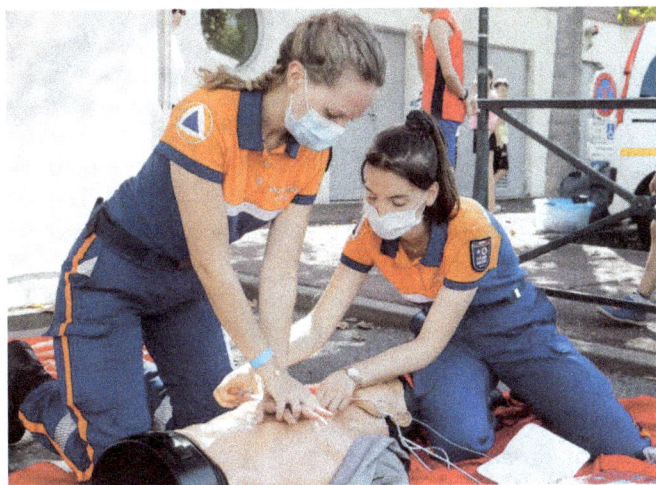

What is First Aid?

First Aid is the provision of initial care for an illness or injury. It is usually performed by a qualified first aider to a sick or injured person until definitive medical treatment can be accessed.

First Aid is the initial assistance or treatment given to a casualty for any injury or sudden illness before the arrival of an ambulance, doctor, or other qualified personnel.

What is the aim of first aid?

Remember three "Ps".
- **P**reservation of life.
- **P**revent worsening the condition.
- **P**romote recovery.

What are your responsibilities as a First Aider?

- Assess the situation quickly and safely and summon appropriate help.
- Protect casualties and others at the scene from possible danger.
- To identify, as far as possible, the nature of illness or injury affecting casualty.
- To give each casualty early and appropriate treatment, treating the most serious condition first.
- To arrange for the casualty's removal to hospital or into the care of a doctor.
- To remain with a casualty until appropriate care is available.
- To report your observations to those taking care of the casualty, and to give further assistance if required.

Casualties should always be treated in the order of priority. Stat the order.

Casualties should always be treated in the order of priority, usually given by the "3 Bs".
- **B**reathing
- **B**leeding
- **B**ones

What does D.R.A.B stands for?

D.R.A.B stands for:
D = Danger
R = Response
A = Airway
B = Breathing

What does C.P.R stands for?

C.P.R stands for **C**ardio **P**ulmonary **R**esuscitation.

What is the aim of Resuscitation?

To prevent damage to the brain and other vital organs, which would occur through lack of oxygen.

Illustrate Rules of Nine for Thermal Burns.

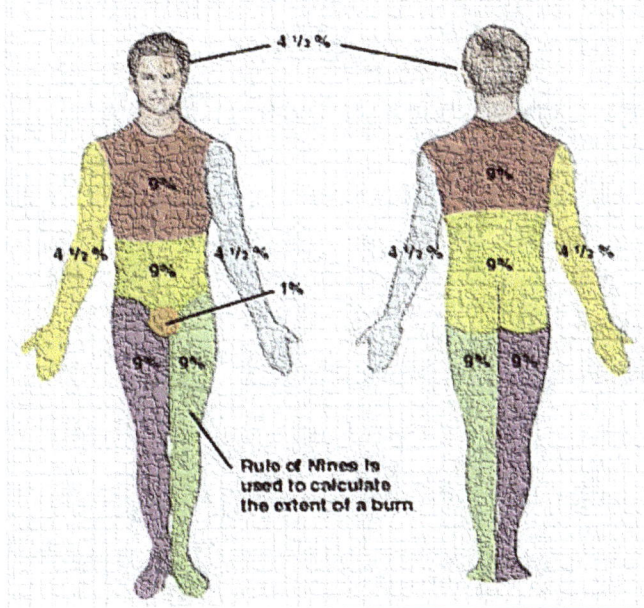

What is the initial first aid treatment for acid burns?

Flood the area with slowly running water for 20 minutes. Gently remove contaminated clothing while flooding the area.

Who must be in charge of a First Aid box?

A responsible or trained person.

To identify if a causality is breathing or not how much time someone should check it for?

Not less than 5 seconds but not more than 10 seconds

How many breaths should be given to a causality before starting C.P.R?

2 breaths of NO more than 2 seconds duration and after that C.P.R should be given in cycles of 30:2 (30 chest compressions plus 2 breaths) in no more than 20 seconds.

Give two methods of treating a person who has fainted?

1. Get the person into fresh air, lay the person flat on their back, raise feet and legs, and loosen tight clothing at neck, waist, and chest.
2. Get the person into fresh air, sit the person down, and loosen tight clothing at neck, waist, and chest, place persons head between their knees.

Name four methods of artificial respiration?

1. Mouth to mouth.
2. Schaeffer.
3. Holgar Nielson.
4. Silvesters.

What is the treatment for a nose bleed? Give four points?

1. Sit the patient up with their head slightly forward.
2. Instruct them to breathe through their mouth.
3. Pinch the soft part of the nose firmly for 10 minutes.
4. Prevent them from swallowing blood.

Name four types of wounds?

- Incised.
- Graze.
- Lacerated.
- Puncture.
- Gun Shot.
- Contused.

If a person's heart is beating faintly should you assist it with heart compression?

No.

What are the two purposes of blood circulation?

1. To carry oxygen to the tissues.
2. To extract carbon dioxide from the tissues.

At what stage can you leave a patient to summon help?

When the patient is breathing normally.

Give two reasons why people who are unconscious are placed in the recovery position?

1. To prevent the tongue falling back and blocking the airways.
2. To prevent vomit lodging at the back of the throat and blocking the airways.

List items that should NOT be applied to serious or severe burns?

Adhesive plaster or tape, lotions, ointments or fats. Fluffy materials e.g. lint.

Give four causes of unconsciousness?

- Stroke Epilepsy
- Drug overdose
- Head injury
- Cardiac arrest
- Poisoning
- Lack of oxygen
- Diabetes
- Alcohol

In First Aid what is meant by the terms "Signs" and "Symptoms"?

Signs - Are the abnormal things such as bleeding, swelling, deformity, raised or irregular pulse – i.e., you see them.

Symptoms - Are sensations that the casualty describes to you such as pain, loss of movement, giddiness, and feeling of heat or cold, - i.e., things you do not see.

What is the medical term given to a severe allergic reaction within the body from a poison?

Anaphylactic Shock.

What instrument is used to measure blood pressure?

A Sphygmomanometer.

Give six signs or symptoms of shock?

- Giddiness or Faintness.
- Coldness.
- Nausea.
- Pallor.
- Cold Clammy Skin.
- Slow Pulse, becoming feeble and rapid.

- Vomiting.
- Unconsciousness.

Name steps in the first aid treatment of shock?

1. Comfort and reassure the casualty.
2. Lay the casualty on a blanket, and keep warm.
3. Keep the head low and turned to one side.
4. Loosen tight clothing to assist circulation.
5. If thirsty, moisten lips with water.
6. Check the pulse, 72 beats per minute.
7. Check breathing rate, 16/18 times per minute.
8. Apply resuscitation, if breathing stops.
9. Get casualty to Doctors care quickly.

In relation to a choking casualty, when should abdominal thrusts NOT be used?

Abdominal thrusts should NOT be used for:
- Pregnant women.
- Overweight casualties.
- Infants.

On arriving at an accident scene, what four steps should you take to control the situation?

- Minimize the danger to yourself and others.
- Get others to assist you.
- Determine the priorities of the situation.
- Call for specialized assistance.

Give four basic pieces of equipment needed for emergency treatment and transport of injured persons?

1. First Aid Box.
2. Stretcher.
3. Blankets.
4. Splints of various sizes.
5. Water container.

What is important when sending a casualty to a doctor or hospital after a works accident? Give four points?

1. The casualty should be accompanied by a note which should refer to the undermentioned.
2. The circumstances of the accident.
3. Detail of materials involved in the accident, e.g. concentration, temperature, time of exposure etc.
4. Details of First Aid administered.

In the case of eye injuries, what should always be done?

They should always be seen by a qualified First Aider or Nurse, and referred to a doctor if necessary.

If somebody is heavily splashed with a corrosive liquid, name two necessary first aid actions?

- Get the person quickly under running water.
- Remove the affected clothing.
- Get professional help if required.

Describe two forms of eyewash bottle?

- Glass bottle with gravity feed.
- Squeezable plastic bottle.

What does an eyewash bottle essentially contain?

Water.

Where are they in body? Humerus, Radius, Ulna, Femur, Tarsals and Metatarsals, Carpals and Metacarpals.

- Humerus is in the upper arm.
- Radius is in the forearm.
- Ulna is in the forearm.
- Femur is in the Thigh.
- Tarsals & metatarsals is in the ankles and feet.
- Carpals & metacarpals is in the wrists and hands.

Give two of the principal types of open wound?

- Incised.
- Lacerated.
- Punctured.

Name two conditions associated with electric shock that may be fatal?

- Asphyxia.
- Serious Burns.
- Fibrillation of the heart.

Other than Electric Shock, what causes asphyxia?

Anything that prevents a supply of fresh air from reaching the lungs.

A person says they feel faint, what two actions must you take?

- Support them until they can sit or lie down.
- Send for a First Aider.

Under what circumstances is it permissible to move a seriously injured person?

If there is further danger by leaving them where they are.

In what area of the body is one likely to sustain a Depressed Fracture?

The Skull.

What is an Antidote?

A substance given to a person who has swallowed a poison to counteract the effects of the poison.

What is an emetic?

A substance given to a person to induce vomiting.

FALL PROTECTION

When Fall Protection is needed?

During roofing, fall protection is always required when the roof edge is more than 10 feet above the ground or other surface.

When fall protection is required on a Low pitched roof?

A roof with a slope of 4:12 or less is a low-pitched roof. Fall protection is required on low-pitched roofs where the fall distance is 10 feet or more such as at the gable end. Fall protection is not normally required on low-pitched roof edge work below 10 feet.

A full-hipped low-pitched roof would not generally require fall protection if the roof edge is below 10 ft.

When fall protection is required on Roofs with more than one level?

Fall protection on roofs with two or more levels is normally required when the level you are working on is 10 feet or more above the ground.

What is the fall protection standard for Hazardous Slopes?

Some roofs are considered "hazardous slopes" when they are steep, slippery or both.

A steep roof is one with a slope greater than 4 in 12. When any roof is so steep or slippery that an uncontrolled fall would likely happen, fall protection is required at 6 feet.

What are types of Fall Protection used during work at height?

- Fall Restraint – equipment that prevents a free fall in the first place.
- Fall Arrest – equipment that stops a free fall in progress (in the middle of the fall).

What are the types of fall restraint system?

There are three types of fall restraint system:
- Personal fall restraint – a body belt or harness connected to an anchor to prevent you from going over the edge of the roof.
- Guardrails.
- Warning line and safety monitor person.

What are the types of fall arrest system?

There are two types of fall arrest system used in roofing.
- Personal Fall Arrest - full body harness is the most common
- Catch Platform – sometimes used on large buildings

Write down requirements for Catch Platforms.

General requirements for Catch Platforms are:
- Must be no lower than 10 ft. from roof edge.
- Must be at least as wide as the fall distance, but never less than 45 inches in width.
- Must have guardrails, toe board and not used for storage.

What qualifies as a full body harness during work at height operations?

- A full body harness is a common fall arrest system used in roofing. A full body harness stops a fall in progress and minimizes the force of the fall to your body.
- Waist belts not allowed because a fall will usually result in injury.
- The attachment point on a full body harness is a D-ring on your upper back.
- It must be a commercial ANSI Class III harness. Recreational climbing harness are not allowed.
- Be sure to use a size that fits you properly.

Why Waist Belts are not safe to use during work at height operations?

Because if you fall, the high force of the fall is concentrated at your waist rather than the 6 points of a full body harness.

What are the required standards for an anchor?

Fall arrest equipment is only as good as the anchor:
- An anchor must be able to withstand 5000 lbs. of force without failing.
- Manufactured anchors must be installed according to manufacturer's instructions.
- Check pre-installed anchors before using.
- In a fall, your life depends on the anchor holding.

A knot can be used to secure a lifeline to an anchor point only when:
- You know the breaking strength of the lifeline.
- And the knot does not decrease the strength of the lifeline below 5000 lbs.

How would you remove material and waste from a height?

By Lowering properly using a hand line, or empty down a chute.

What two precautions are necessary in an area where work may take place on a fragile roof?

1. Warning notices must be displayed warning personnel of the fragile roof condition.
2. Crawling boards or ladders must be used when working on fragile roofs.

What precautions are necessary in an area where work may take place on a sloping roof?

Crawling boards or ladders must be used when working on a sloping roof.

Name the two most obvious safeguards for persons when working over water?

Life jackets are a must. Plus a boat should be in the vicinity for any emergency situation.

How to ensure that equipment used for fall protection are safe to use?

Do the following to ensure their safe use:
- Inspect for wear and damage before use.
- Remove from service after a fall for inspection.
- Don't use to lift materials.
- Don't attach to guardrails or hoists.

What to look for when inspecting fall arrest equipment?

Look for the following defects in equipment and remove them from service in order to ensure personnel safety.
- Webbing - Cuts, tears, abrasion, fraying, stretching, mold, chemical damage.
- D-rings - Cracks, breaks corrosion, rough edges.
- Tongue-buckle - Distortions, added holes, broken grommets.
- Ropes - Abrasion, internal damage.

What are the general requirements for a fall protection work plan?

The employer shall develop and implement a written fall protection work plan including each area of the work place where the employees are assigned and where fall hazards of 6 feet or more exist.

The fall protection work plan shall:
- Identify all fall hazards in the work area.
- Describe the method of fall arrest or fall restraint to be provided.
- Describe the correct procedures for the assembly, maintenance, inspection, and disassembly of the fall protection system to be used.
- Describe the correct procedures for the handling, storage, and securing of tools and materials.
- Describe the method of providing overhead protection for workers who may be in, or pass through the area below the work site.
- Describe the method for prompt, safe removal of injured workers.
- Be available on the job site for inspection by the concerned authorities/department.

Prior to permitting employees into areas where fall hazards exist the employer shall:
- Ensure that employees are trained and instructed in the items described above.
- Inspect fall protection devices and systems to ensure compliance with required regulations.

Training of employees:
- The employer shall ensure that employees are trained as required by this section. Training shall be documented and shall be available on the job site.

When a fall protection work plan is developed?

Before start of work where fall hazards exists in a work site. Workers are not allowed to enter and start their work till development and implementation of a fall protection work plan. It's required by law.

What is the ladder rule?

Ladders must be stabilized and extend at least 3 feet above the roof edge. Both hands must be free when climbing a ladder.

What is defined as a sloping roof?

One where the pitch is more than 10 degrees.

Name two precautions which must be taken to safe guard workers when working on heights if scaffolding is impossible to use?

1. Use of Safety Nets.
2. Use of Safety Belts.

What type of protection is a must for everyone on a construction site?

A Safety Helmet

How would you remove material and waste from a height?

Lower properly using a hand line, or empty down a chute.

What 2 precautions are necessary in an area where work may take place on a fragile roof?

1. Warning notices must be displayed warning personnel of the fragile roof condition.
2. Crawling boards or ladders must be used when working on fragile roofs.

What precautions are necessary in an area where work may take place on a sloping roof?

Crawling boards or ladders must be used when working on a sloping roof.

S.C.B.A

What is S.C.B.A?

S.C.B.A is an abbreviation for Self Contained Breathing Apparatus. It provides respiratory protection when working in toxic or unbreathable atmospheres.

The S.C.B.A together with full firefighting clothing, is a part of the framework of the firefighters' Personal Protective Equipment.

What is Harness Frame?

The Harness Frame is the rigid base to which the harness straps and pressure reducer assembly are attached. Its main purpose is to hold the cylinder which is done by means of an adjustable cylinder band and a locking tab.

What is Harness Assembly?

The Harness Assembly consists of two adjustable shoulder straps and an adjustable waist belt with a quick release. This waist belt rests on the hips of the wearer and distributes most of the weight of the S.C.B.A to that area.

The shoulder straps have pockets through which the low pressure hose and the remote gauge line pass.

What are the capacities of gas cylinders in S.C.B.A?

Capacity	Gas Pressure	Duration
45 CUBIC FT OF AIR	2216 P.S.I	30 MIN.
45 CUBIC FT OF AIR	4500 P.S.I	30 MIN.
66 CUBIC FT OF AIR	3000 P.S.I	45 MIN.
87 CUBIC FT OF AIR	4500 P.S.I	60 MIN.

S.C.B.A breathing cylinder is made of what materials?

Cylinders are constructed of an aluminum shell and are wrapped with layers of fiberglass, which strengthen and protect the shell. The low weight and high pressurization of the cylinder is dependent upon the aluminum / fiberglass composition.

What type of Air is in S.C.B.A cylinder?

It contains purified air.

Describe the breathing apparatus conditions known as "Demand" and "Positive pressure".

Demand Condition: In this condition the demand valve meters air into the face piece when the wearer breathes in.

Positive Pressure: In this condition the face piece is under slight positive pressure at all times. Hence fume & smoke is prevented from entering the face piece, unlike demand which could allow fume & smoke into the face piece.

What is the average consumption of air in a compressed air breathing apparatus?

40 liters per minute.

What are Emergency Breathing Procedures?

Skip Breathing
- Firefighter inhales
- Holds breath for as long as it takes to exhale
- Then exhales
- Repeats breathing process

Cuts Respirations in Half

Controlled Breathing
- Firefighter consciously slows down breathing
- Inhale through nose exhale through mouth

S.C.B.A puts limitation on its wearer. What are they?

The wearer abilities are limited while using S.C.B.A by:
- Limited visibility
- Decreased ability to communicate
- Increased weight
- Air capacity of cylinder
- Decreased mobility

Improper use of the S.C.B.A may result in personal injury or death if?

- Used without proper training
- Disregard of instructions
- Disregard of warnings
- Failure to maintain the unit
- Failure to inspect the unit

PERSONAL PROTECTIVE EQUIPMENT

What is P.P.E?

Personal Protective Equipment (P.P.E) refers to protective clothing, helmets, goggles, or other garment designed to protect the wearer's body from injury by blunt impacts, electrical hazards, heat, chemicals & infections etc., for job-related occupational safety & health purposes.

Personal Protective Equipment, or PPE, is designed to protect workers from serious workplace injuries or illnesses resulting from contact with chemical, radiological, physical, electrical, mechanical, or other workplace hazards. Besides face shields, safety glasses, hard hats, & safety shoes, protective equipment includes a variety of devices and garments such as goggles, coveralls, gloves, vests, earplugs, and respirators.

When P.P.Es are required?

P.P.Es are required when all feasible engineering & administrative controls to eliminate & reduce hazards have been used & the risk level remains high enough to necessitate the use of appropriate P.P.E.

Give examples of P.P.Es for different body parts.

- Eye - safety glasses, goggles
- Face - face shields
- Head - hard hats
- Feet - safety shoes
- Hands and arms - gloves
- Bodies - vests
- Hearing - earplugs, earmuffs

Employees required to wear PPEs must be trained to know at-least what?

They must be trained to know at least the following:
- When PPE is necessary
- What type of PPE is necessary
- How to properly put on, take off, adjust, and wear
- Limitations of the PPE
- Proper care, maintenance, useful life and disposal

Items that must be provided when corrosive liquids are being handled?

- Suitable Gloves.
- Goggles or Visors.
- Suitable Overalls.
- Suitable Footwear.

What does R.P.E stands for?

Respiratory Protective Equipment.

Occasions when eye protection should be worn, when there is risk of injury to the eyes?

- Flying Particles.
- Splashing with chemicals.
- Welding or Brazing.
- Burning.
- Radiation.

What are the two essential factors about a helmet to be worn while blasting materials?

- It must be totally enclosed.
- It must be of the air-supplied type.

What protective clothing is necessary when working with acids and corrosive materials, and what is the correct way of wearing it?

- Full Face Visor Overall. PVC/Rubber Gloves. Rubber Boots. PVC Apron/Acid Suit. Glasses/Goggles.
- Glasses under visor. Acid Suit Sleeves over gloves. Trouser Legs over Boots.

What are some of the causes of eye injuries?

- Molten metal that might splash.
- Acids & other caustic liquid chemicals that might splash.
- Blood and other potentially infectious body fluids that might splash, spray or splatter.
- Intense light such as that created by welding & lasers.
- Dust and other flying particles, such as metal shavings or sawdust.

Why you should remove gloves before goggles?

Because to prevent contamination of the face or eyes.

Will any type of two eyepiece goggles do for welders?

No, they must be the correct color to protect against ultra violet light.

Describe safety spectacles and its uses.

- They are made from metal/plastic safety frames.
- Most operations require side shields.
- They are used for moderate impact from particles produced by such jobs as carpentry, woodworking, grinding, and scaling.

What is the use of goggles as a P.P.E?

Goggles protect eyes, eye sockets, and the facial area immediately surrounding the eyes from impact, dust, & splashes.

What is the use of welding shields as a P.P.E?

Welding shields protect eyes from burns caused by infrared or intense radiant light, and protect face and eyes from flying sparks, metal spatter and slag chips produced during welding, brazing, soldering and cutting.

When should eye protection be worn?

At any time when there is danger to the eyes.

What are some of the causes of head injuries?

- Contact with exposed electrical conductors.
- Falling objects.
- Bumping head against fixed objects, such as exposed pipes or beams.

What protection does face shields provide?

They protect the face from nuisance dusts and potential splashes or sprays of hazardous liquids. But do not protect employees from impact hazards.

What are classes of Hard Hats?

Class A
- General Service (e.g., mining, building construction, shipbuilding, lumbering, and manufacturing).
- Good impact protection but limited voltage protection.

Class B
- Best for Electrical Work.
- Protect against falling objects and high-voltage shock and burns.

Class C
- Designed for comfort, offer limited protection.
- Protects heads that may bump against fixed objects, but do not protect against falling objects or electrical shock.

Why wear hard hats on building sites?

To get protection against falling objects and striking the head on structures.

What are some of the causes of foot injuries?

- Heavy objects such as barrels or tools that might roll onto or fall on employees' feet.
- Molten metal that might splash on feet.
- Sharp objects such as nails or spikes that might pierce the soles or uppers of ordinary shoes.
- Hot or wet surfaces.
- Slippery surfaces.

What standards Safety Shoes should have?

- They should have impact-resistant toes and heat-resistant soles that protect against hot surfaces common in roofing, paving, and hot metal industries.
- Must have metal insoles to protect against puncture wounds.
- Must be designed to be electrically conductive for use in explosive atmospheres, or non-conductive to protect from workplace electrical hazards.
- May have Metatarsal Guards which are a part of the shoes or strapped to the outside of shoes to protect the instep from impact and compression.

How do you test a canister respirator for air tightness?

Fit closely, squeeze the air tube and take a deep breath.

What clothing is normally worn when there is intense radiant heat?

Aluminized heat resistant clothing is normally worn when there is intense radiant heat.

What are some of the causes of body injuries?

- Splashes of hot metals and other hot liquids
- Impacts from tools, machinery, and materials
- Cuts
- Hazardous chemicals
- Contact with potentially infectious materials, like blood

- Radiation
- Intense heat

What are some of the hand injuries you need to guard against?

- Burns
- Bruises
- Abrasions
- Cuts
- Punctures
- Fractures
- Amputations
- Chemical Exposures

Describe different types of gloves.

- Butyl provides the highest permeation resistance to gas or water vapors; frequently used for ketones (M.E.K., Acetone) and esters (Amyl Acetate, Ethyl Acetate).
- Norfoil laminate resists permeation and breakthrough by an array of toxic/hazardous chemicals.
- Viton is highly resistant to permeation by chlorinated and aromatic solvents.
- Nitrile provides protection against a wide variety of solvents, harsh chemicals, fats and petroleum products and also provides excellent resistance to cuts, snags, punctures and abrasions.
- Kevlar protects against cuts, slashes, and abrasion.
- Stainless steel mesh protects against cuts and lacerations.

CHEMICALS

Chemicals can enter your body through how many routes?

Chemicals can enter your body through following ways.
- Inhalation
- Injection
- Ingestion
- Absorption

What are four basic rules of chemical safety?

The four rules of chemical safety are:
- Don't buy or store chemicals you do not need.
- Store chemicals in their original container. – The original container was designed to hold the chemical without degrading. The original container will have an accurate label. Serious injury can result when people try to identify chemicals with missing or uncertain labels by smelling, tasting or touching.
- Always wear appropriate safety gear and work in a safe environment.
- Always dispose of chemicals safely.

Chemicals can cause injury/illness in how many ways?

Chemicals can cause injury/illness through:
- Chemical Burns (strong acids, strong bases).
- Heat Burns (flammable materials).
- Poisoning (many chemicals are damaging or fatal if taken internally, whether by swallowing, injection, or leaching through skin).
- Chronic illness (long-term exposure to even low doses of certain chemical agents can lead to chronic health conditions).

What is chronic disease?

The term chronic is usually applied when the course of the disease lasts for more than three months. Common chronic diseases include asthma, cancer, diabetes and HIV/AIDS.

What is MSDS?

MSDS stands for **M**aterial **S**afety **D**ata **S**heets.

What does MSDS contains?

MSDS contains all the information available about particular chemical present. For example it may contain information like in the form (but not limited to) below about a chemical:
- Section 1 - Product and Company Identification
- Section 2 - Composition/Information on Ingredients
- Section 3 - Hazards Identification Including Emergency Overview
- Section 4 - First Aid Measures
- Section 5 - Fire Fighting Measures
- Section 6 - Accidental Release Measures
- Section 7 - Handling and Storage
- Section 8 - Exposure Controls & Personal Protection
- Section 9 - Physical & Chemical Properties
- Section 10 - Stability & Reactivity Data
- Section 11 - Toxicological Information
- Section 12 - Ecological Information
- Section 13 - Disposal Considerations
- Section 14 - MSDS Transport Information
- Section 15 - Regulatory Information
- Section 16 - Other Information

By Law they should always be present with a chemical.

What are general categories of chemicals?

- Acids
- Bases
- Flammable
- Oxidizers
- Pyrophoric Substances
- Light-Sensitive Chemicals
- Carcinogens

If a solution has a pH 4 value. Is it an acid or alkaline?

It's an Acid.

If a solution has a pH 11 value. Is it an acid or alkaline?

It's an Alkaline.

How would you ensure safe storage of strong acids?

Some general precautions for strong acids are:
- Store large bottles of acids on low shelf or in acid cabinets.
- Segregate oxidizing acids from organic acids, flammables and combustible materials.
- Segregate acids from bases and active metals such as sodium, potassium, etc.
- Use bottle carrier for transporting acid bottles.
- Have spill control pillows or acid neutralizers available in case of spill.

Give two reasons why chemical containers should be clearly marked with an approved code?

- To identify the contents.
- To comply with regulations.

State the height that should a fixed vessel containing a dangerous material be fenced up?

3 feet or 0.92 m.

In a mixture of petrol and water, which liquid will be on top?

Petrol will be on top due to density differences.

In a mixture of alcohol and water, which liquid will be on top?

Neither as they will mix up.

What does the risk phrase R45 mean?

It means that it can cause cancer. It's a carcinogen.

What does the risk phrase R40 mean?

It means that there is a possible risk of irreversible effects.

What gas can be formed if acid comes in contact with Sodium Cyanide?

Hydrogen Cyanide.

How would you ensure safe storage of strong bases?

Some general precautions for strong bases are:
- Store bases and acids separate from one another.
- Store solutions of inorganic hydroxides in polyethylene containers.
- Have spill control pillows or caustic neutralizers available for spills.

Can you name the term used to describe substances that pose a hazard to the environment?

Eco-toxic.

The word used to describe a chemical reaction which absorbs heat?

Endothermic Reaction.

The word used to describe a chemical reaction which gives out heat?

Exothermic Reaction.

What is the difference between toxic and toxicity?

Toxic means the ability to cause harmful health effects. And Toxicity is a measure of the degree to which something is toxic.

Name three of the factors on which the severity of a chemical burn depends?

- Concentration of the chemical
- Duration of contact
- Area or extent of the burn.

What does the term S.T.E.L mean?

Short Term Exposure Limit.

Occupational Exposure Limits (OEL's) are normally expressed in terms of applying to either short or longer times of exposure. What are the two time periods that may be involved?

15 Minutes or 8 Hours.

What is a fume cupboard?

It is a specially ventilated and enclosed area in which laboratory work with harmful gases and vapors can be carried out safely.

How would you ensure safe storage of flammable materials?

Some general precautions for flammable materials are:
- Store in approved safety cans or cabinets.
- Segregate from oxidizing acids and oxidizers.
- Keep away from any source of ignition: flames, heat or sparks.
- Know where firefighting equipment is stored and how to use.
- If volatile flammable liquids are stored in a refrigerator it must be in an explosion-proof (lab-safe) refrigerator.

When Threshold Limit Values are given on a data sheet for a substance, give two important facts that must not be assumed?

The T.L.V. is not an index of relative Toxicity. And the T.L.V. does not indicate the relative hazardous nature of a substance.

What hazards result from a mercury spill, and how should these hazards be dealt with?

Being highly toxic, it is a significant respiratory hazard. So it should be collected with appropriate equipment or chemically neutralized.

Name two materials that can ignite when in contact with water?

Sodium Chloride & Mercury.

What is the difference between carcinogen, carcinogenic & carcinogenicity?

- A Carcinogen is a substance that can cause cancer.
- Carcinogenic means able to cause cancer.
- Carcinogenicity is the ability of a substance to cause cancer.

Give 4 Hazards which face cryogenic fluid users?

Frost bite, respiratory ailments, chemical burns & some react violently when combined with their surroundings.

Is the sniffing of chemicals a safe means of identification of them?

Chemicals should never be sniffed as a means of identification, as some chemicals can be harmful even below the threshold of smell.

If you were told a solution was pH 7. Would it be acid or alkaline?

It will be Neutral. Water has a pH value around 7.

How would Oxidizers be stored in a workplace?

- Store in a cool, dry place.
- Keep away from flammable and combustible materials, such as paper or wood.
- Keep away from reducing agents such as zinc, alkaline metals, formic acid.

How would you neutralize spilt acid?

Use an alkali or plenty of water to up the pH value towards 7 as much as is practicable.

What is a Pyrophoric Substance? And how would you store them?

A pyrophoric substance is a substance that will ignite spontaneously in air. Examples are iron sulfide & many reactive metals like uranium, when powdered or sliced thin. They are often water-reactive as well & will ignite when they contact water or humid air. So store:
- In a cool place.
- In containers that omit air.

Beware of low humidity circumstances in which static electricity may be high.

Is Carbon tetrachloride a safe cleaning fluid, qualify your answer?

No it is not a safe cleaning fluid. It is toxic in nature.

What does the risk phrase R61 mean?

It means it may cause harm to the unborn child.

How would you describe a substance which may on contact with living tissue destroy it, and what sign is used to indicate this substance?

Corrosive - This is depicted by a test tube pouring drops of liquid onto a material with fumes rising from the material.

Give the meaning of the four following chemical industry terms, Aqueous, Immiscible, Inert, and Emulsion?

- Aqueous: Contains Water
- Immiscible: Does not mix
- Inert: Non- Reactive
- Emulsion: Suspension in liquid

The term LD 50 is often recorded in data dealing with toxic chemicals. What does it signify?

Lethal Dose - 50% Kill. i.e., the dose that killed 50% of the test animals.

What does O.E.L.V stand for?

Occupational Exposure Limit Value.

What are light sensitive chemicals? And how would you store them?

Chemicals whose composition can change if exposed to light.
To Store:
- Avoid exposure to light.
- Store in amber bottles in a cool, dry place.

List four possible health effects of hazardous substances?

- Sensitization
- Asthma
- Skin irritation or dermatitis
- Cancer Poisoning Burns

Name four flammable gases.

- Acetylene
- Ethylene
- Hydrogen Cyanide
- Propylene.

Name three cryogenic fluids.

Hydrogen, Oxygen & Nitrogen.

What do you understand by the following terms?

- **Acute Toxicity**
- **Chronic Toxicity**

- Acute Toxicity refers to the situation where a substance produces harmful effects quickly i.e. Seconds, Minutes, and Hours.
- Chronic Toxicity refers to the situation where a substance produces harmful effects in a long period of time i.e. Months or years.

Both Sodium and Phosphorus ignite spontaneously in air. How should they be stored, and can they be stored together?

Sodium must be stored under paraffin, Phosphorus under water. They should not be stored near each other as confusion would be dangerous - Sodium reacts violently with water.

What is a carcinogen? And what are its safety precautions?

A carcinogen is any substance, radiation that is an agent directly involved in causing cancer.

Safety precautions would be:
- Label all containers as Cancer Suspect Agents.
- Store according to hazardous nature of chemicals, e.g., flammable, corrosive.
- When necessary, store securely.

ELECTRICITY

What is Electricity?

Electricity is the flow of electrons.

What is Ohm's law?

In 1827, George Simon Ohm discovered that the flow of electric current was directly proportional to the applied voltage and inversely proportional to the "resistance" of the wires or cables (conductors) and the load. This discovery became known as Ohm's Law.

Write down formula for Ohm' law.

The Current in Amperes (I) is equal to the electromotive force, or Voltage (V) divided by the Resistance (R) in "ohms".

$$\text{Current (I)} = \frac{\text{Voltage (V)}}{\text{Resistance (R)}}$$

Hence it is proved! $I = V/R$

Write down electrical hazards.

Electricity has three main hazards. They are:
1. Electric shock
2. Arc flash
3. Arc blast

What is an electric shock?

An electric shock occurs when a person comes into contact with an electrical energy source. Electrical energy flows through a portion of the body causing a shock.

Explain Arc Flash and Arc Blast.

An arc flash (or arc blast) is a type of electrical explosion that results from a low impedance connection to ground or another voltage phase in an electrical system.

Severity of shock depends on what factors?

Severity of a shock depends on following factors:
- Path of current through the body.
- Amount of current flowing through the body.
- Length of time the body is in the circuit.

Why use fuses in an electrical circuit?

To give protection from circuit overloads.

What is a circuit breaker?

A device used as a means of starting or stopping an electrical current flow.

What are safety precautions if electrocution occurs?

- Call for help.
- DO NOT touch the victim or the conductor.
- Shut off the current at the control box.
- If the shutoff is not immediately available, use a non-conducting material to free the victim.
- If necessary and you know how, begin CPR (Cardio pulmonary resuscitation) when current is stopped.
- In dealing with electricity, never exceed your expertise.

What are the clues that electrical hazards exist in a workplace?

- Tripped circuit breakers or blown fuses.
- Warm tools, wires, cords, connections, or junction boxes.
- GFCI that shuts off a circuit.
- Worn or frayed insulation around wire or connection.

Give two ways to make an electrically driven machine safe to do maintenance work on?

1. Lock out the switch with own lock.
2. Remove the fuses.

How is a double insulated appliance identified?

A double insulated appliance is marked with two squares one inside the other.

What is grounding?

Grounding creates a low-resistance path from a tool to the earth to disperse unwanted current.
When a short or lightning occurs, energy flows to the ground, protecting you from electrical shock, injury and death.

Why is grounding of equipment necessary?

To ensure protective action results if the metal work becomes live due to a fault.

When an Earth Leakage Circuit Breaker is combined with an Excess Current Operated Circuit Breaker, what protection is given to the circuit?

The circuit is protected against earth faults and overloads.

What causes Static Electricity?

Movement and friction of materials which may be solids, liquids or gases.

Static Electricity is produced when electrons are displaced in the surface of material. Give two common causes of a buildup of a static electricity charge?

1. The flow of solids.
2. The flow of liquids.

What is the basic thing that should be done if there is a risk of Static Electricity builds up?

Earth the relevant equipment.

Give two ways of identifying fuses in relation to electrical load.

1. By Color.
2. By Size.
3. Capacity on Fuse.

Give reasons for keeping power cables off the floor?

- Damage to Cables.
- A Tripping Hazard.

If a fault develops in a portable electric tool, what action should you take?

You must cease to use it, and report it to your supervisor.

What type of electrical equipment is necessary where there is a risk of fire or explosion from fumes?

Equipment suitably classified for the exposure.

In Health and Safety Legislation, how is high voltage defined?

That exceeds 1,000 volts on A.C & 1,500 volts in D.C.

Name four requirements of a battery charging room?

1. It must be free of smoking or naked flames.
2. It must have adequate ventilation.
3. It must have adequate suitable fire extinguishers.
4. It must have suitably classified electrical fittings.

Name four main requirements of an Electric Isolation Request Permit?

1. To nominate the precise plant to be isolated.
2. To nominate a date and time for the isolation.
3. To nominate the type of isolation required i.e., fuses or cables etc.
4. To get an acknowledgement when the isolation is complete.
5. To de-isolate and restore power to the equipment when safe to do so.

Where a high voltage transformer or switchgear outside a building is to be protected by fencing what minimum height of fence is required?

2.4 meters (8 feet approx.)

What is the purpose of Insulation Resistance Tests?

To ensure that phase and neutral conductors are not 'leaking' to earth.

What is the purpose of Continuity Resistance Tests?

To ensure that where fitted ring cables (such as socket circuits) are intact.

What is the purpose of Earth Fault Loop Impedance (EFLI) tests?

They are carried out to verify that earthing characteristics are satisfactory.

What is the purpose of checking Tripping times?

To see if the tripping time of residual current devices (RCD) are within acceptable time limits.

What is the purpose of protective devices in electrical circuits?

To protect against overload to protect against faults.

Within the context of electrical safety what is the meaning of the term isolation?

Isolation means the disconnection and separation of electrical equipment from every source of electrical energy in such a way that the disconnection and separation is secure

What three steps should be taken after the operation of a Residual Current Device (R.C.D.)?

1. Check the appliance connected to the circuit breaker for fault or defect.
2. Correct the fault or defect.
3. Re-set the circuit breaker in the positive mode.

Name few types of protective devices used in an electrical circuit?

1. Fuse
2. Miniature Circuit breaker (MCB)
3. Residual Current Device (RCD)
4. Residual Current Circuit breakers (RCCB)
5. Residual Current Circuit breakers with Overload protection (RCBO)
6. Magnetic Hydraulic Circuit breakers
7. Thermal Circuit breakers
8. Thermal Magnetic Circuit breakers

What is the difference between an overload current and a fault current?

An overload current is the application of a current greater than the design current resulting in the disruption of the circuit protective device.
Fault current is one generated by the rapid discharge of energy to earth through a mechanical fault on a system resulting in a substantial rise and rapid disconnection by the circuit protective device.

What two conditions can occur to the heart with electric shock, and what action should be taken for each condition?

1. Cardiac arrest, (the heart stops beating and blood is no longer circulated). Treatment - immediate CPR.
9. Ventricular fibrillation, (the heart's electrical activity becomes disordered) Treatment - use defibrillator followed by CPR.

What is GFCI?

GFCI stands for Ground Fault Circuit Interrupter.

What is flameproof electrical equipment?

Electrical equipment which can be used with safety in a flammable atmosphere without the risk of causing a fire.

Give two methods of protecting yourself from risk of shock to earth which do not involve electrical trip devices?

- Use rubber mats.
4. Wear rubber boots.

What is bonding and why is it important?

Bonding is the process of interconnecting all exposed metalwork to eliminate voltage differences (potential) between parts of the metalwork.
It reduces the risk of electric shock and the risk of static electricity build up and is particularly important in livestock buildings, milking parlors and in bathrooms, etc.

In relation to electrical safety, all socket outlets should be protected by an RCD with an operating current not exceeding?

30mA.

What is meager test?

The insulation break down test is known as meager test.

Why meager test is necessary for electric tools?

A tool having subjected to harsh use at site needs to be tested for insulation break down to avoid possible electric shock.

Why dead man switch should be used on electric tools?

To cut off the power supply to the tool in emergency.

Give four safety checks recommended before connecting an appliance to a mains supply?

1. Check appliance name plate voltage and frequency is matched to supply potential.
2. Ensure socket and tool are switched off before plugging in.
3. Check cable and plug are in good condition.
4. Ensure that the cable is clear of the work.

Poor lighting results in 4 well identified undesirable consequences. Can you name them?

1. Fatigue.
2. Errors.
3. Stress.
4. Accidents.

The maintenance of a well-designed lighting system at its peak efficiency can be dependent on four essential maintenance tasks. Can you name them?

- Replacement of spent bulbs.
- Correct bulb replacement.
- Regular cleaning of lamps.
- Regular cleaning of windows.

The degree of illumination required to enable any specific task to be performed with relative ease and safety depends upon five factors. Name them.

1. Size of object.
2. Speed of movement.
3. Duration of task.
4. Brightness contrasts.
- Color.

What is the name of the effect that makes a rotating shaft appear stationary under certain lighting conditions?

Stroboscopic Effect.

Name two types of fire extinguisher that can be used on an electrical fire.

- Dry Powder
- CO_2
- FM 200

List type of extinguisher that should not be used in electrical fire.

Water

FOOD SAFETY

Who is a PIC?

The Person in Charge (PIC) in any food establishment will be the person who has the overall responsibility for running that location during the entire time of operation.
A PIC will have an active role in managing food safety in a food establishment.

What is HACCP?

HACCP is an abbreviation of **H**azard **A**nalysis **C**ritical **C**ontrol **P**oints.
A food safety management system which identifies, evaluates and controls hazards which are significant for food safety.

What are the 7 PIC Principles of Responsibility (CATCHES)?

- **C**ross-contamination (prevent)
- **A**ctive Managerial Control (apply)
- **T**ime/Temperature Control (ensure)
- **C**leaning and disinfecting
- **H**ygiene of personnel
- **E**mergencies (complaints, recall, power failure)
- **S**ources (approved)

What are High-risk foods?

High-risk foods are ready-to-eat foods, which support the multiplication of harmful bacteria and include most cooked foods. These foods are usually proteins. Examples are:
- Cooked meat and cooked poultry
- Cooked meat products such as pâtés, gravy, stews, meat pies and stock
- Milk, cream, soft cheese, custards and dairy produce
- Eggs and products made from raw eggs, e.g. mayonnaise, desserts
- Shellfish and other seafood especially oysters, prawns and crabs
- Cooked rice

What are Low-risk foods?

Bacteria cannot multiply in dry food or food containing high concentrations of sugar, salt, acid and other preservatives. These foods are known as low-risk. They include:
- Cereals, dried pasta, bread, biscuits, jam, canned food and crisps.
- When water is added to dried food such as milk powder it becomes high-risk and must be stored under refrigeration or used immediately.

How Raw foods to be cooked can be contaminated?

Raw foods are likely to already be contaminated with large numbers of food poisoning organisms and must be kept separate from ready-to-eat foods.
The food poisoning organisms will be destroyed by thorough cooking.

How Ready-to-eat raw foods can be contaminated?

Raw foods such as salads or fruit may be contaminated with bacteria and viruses which may cause illness even when present in very low numbers. They must always be washed in running water before eating.

What are typical signs of food spoilage?

- Off-odors
- Discoloration
- Slime/stickiness
- Mould growth
- Changes in texture, e.g. dry or spongy
- Unusual taste, e.g. sour
- The production of gas
- Blown cans or leaking packs

What are the advantages (benefits) of GOOD hygiene?

A food business has a LEGAL and MORAL obligation to produce safe food and the PIC will hold the primary responsibility.
- A good reputation – customer confidence
- Improved food safety standards
- Compliance with food safety legislation
- Reduced risk of food poisoning

- Longer shelf life
- Good working conditions, higher staff morale and reduced turnover of staff
- Increased productivity
- Brand protection

What are the disadvantages (costs) of POOR hygiene?

- Poor morale – high staff turnover A bad reputation/brand damage
- Food contamination and customer complaints
- Fines and legal costs resulting from prosecution
- Closure of business, prohibition of processes
- Civil action from ill or annoyed customers
- Increased risk of food poisoning deaths and suffering
- Increased risk of pest infestation
- Waste food due to spoilage

What is a pathogen?

A bacterium which causes illness is called pathogen.

Which types of food most readily support the growth of pathogenic bacteria?

Low acid, protein-based and moist.

Which control method is used to destroy pathogenic bacteria?

Cooking food thoroughly.

What factors affect bacterial multiplication?

Nutrients, pH, available water and temperature.

Which temperature ranges provides the best conditions for the growth of most food poisoning bacteria?

20ºC - 50ºC

After cooking meat, which is to be served cold, why should it be rapidly cooled?

To prevent spores from germinating in food.

On which of the following are food poisoning bacteria most likely to be found?

1. Food which has been thoroughly cooked
2. Oven surfaces
3. Plates that have been in a dishwasher
4. Containers used for defrosting chicken

Containers used for defrosting chicken.

What are common vehicles of food poisoning organisms?

Cloths, hands, food-contact surfaces and hand-contact surfaces.

What are the common sources of food poisoning bacteria?

People, raw food, pests, sewage.

Which of the following is likely to result in an allergenic hazard?

1. Storing chemicals with food
2. Using softwood worktops
3. Storing food under refrigeration
4. Poor communication between customers and staff

Poor communication between customers and staff.

Which of the following practices is most likely to result in the chemical contamination of food?

1. Storing disinfectants in a dry food store
2. Not washing hands after using the toilet
3. Using an electric fly killer
4. Washing a lettuce in tap water

Storing disinfectants in a dry food store

List few Foodborne diseases.

- Campylobacter enteritis
- Escherichia coli O157
- Norovirus
- Listeria (refrigerator)
- Typhoid/paratyphoid
- Hepatitis A
- Dysentery
- Parasites

How can we prevent food poisoning?

- Break the food poisoning chain
- Food poisoning rarely occurs because of a single isolated mistake
- Control involves the implementation of good hygiene practices and HACCP
- Remove sources
- Prevent contamination of food
- Prevent multiplication of bacteria
- Destroy bacteria

How Food poisoning occurs?

Food poisoning usually results from eating contaminated food. Food poisoning is usually an acute illness resulting from eating contaminated or poisonous food. It excludes allergies to food or toxins. The symptoms normally include one or more of the following: abdominal pain, diarrhea, vomiting, fever and nausea.

The incubation period (onset time) for bacterial food poisoning is usually how much?

1 to 36 hours.

What is Gastroenteritis?

This term is used to refer to an inflammation of the stomach and intestinal tract that normally results in diarrhea.

Who are Carriers?

Carriers are people who show no symptoms of illness but excrete food poisoning or foodborne pathogens which may contaminate food, for example, salmonellae or shigellae. Organisms may be excreted intermittently.

What are Commensals?

Commensals are bacteria which live on or in the body without causing illness. Most bacteria on the body are commensals and are part of the normal flora.
For example, some species of staphylococcus are found on the skin and in the mouth or nose. Other species are transient and may cause skin infections, such as boils. If harmful species of staphylococcus are transferred to high-risk food, they may cause illness.

What are moulds?

Moulds are aerobic chlorophyll-free fungi which produce thread-like filaments (hyphae) and form a branched network of mycelium. Moulds, which may be black, white or of various colors, will grow on most foods, whether moist or dry, acid or alkaline and high in salt or sugar concentrations. The optimum growth temperature is usually 20°C to 30°C, although they will grow well over a wide range of temperatures and may cause problems in refrigerators. Growth has been recorded as low as -10°C. High humidities and fluctuating temperatures accelerate mould growth.

How do you explain yeasts?

Yeasts are microscopic fungi which reproduce by budding. Most yeasts grow best in the presence of oxygen, although fermentative types may grow slowly anaerobically. The majority of yeasts prefer acid foods (pH 4 to 4.5) with a reasonable level of available moisture.
However, many yeasts will grow in high concentrations of sugar and salt. The optimum growth temperature for yeast is around 25°C to 30°C with a maximum of around 47°C. Some yeasts can grow slowly at 0°C and below. Yeasts are used in the manufacture of foods such as bread, beer and vinegar.
However, they cause spoilage of many foods including jam, fruit juice, honey, meats etc.

What are Protozoa?

Protozoa are single-celled organisms which form the basis of the food chain. They live in most habitats such as oceans, soil and decaying matter.
Some are pathogenic and usually result in waterborne outbreaks. They do not multiply in food but their cysts may remain infectious in foods for a long time. Furthermore, they have a low infective dose, i.e. only small numbers of cysts are required to cause illness. Examples are: Cryptosporidium parvum and Giardia lamblia.

Which of the following is most likely to result in food poisoning?

a) Pasteurized (heat treated) milk unrefrigerated for 4 hours
b) Cooked meat contaminated with pathogens
c) Raw meat contaminated with pathogens
d) A product made with eggs that have been thoroughly cooked

Cooked meat contaminated with pathogens.

Viruses differ from food poisoning bacteria because?

They are more likely to be passed from person to person and only require small numbers to cause illness.

Which groups of people are most at risk of food poisoning?

The elderly, pregnant women and babies.

What is the faecal-oral route?

Pathogens in faeces > hands > food > eaten.

What is most important to reduce the risk of food poisoning, before starting work?

To wash hands properly.

Which of the following statements is true?
a) It is a legal requirement for food handlers to report an illness which may contaminate food
b) A food handler with typhoid can return to work 48 hours after symptoms have gone
c) Food handlers always need a certificate from the doctor before returning to work after suffering from diarrhoea
d) Viruses causing gastroenteritis multiply in food

It is a legal requirement for food handlers to report an illness which may contaminate food

What should a PIC do when a food handler returns to work following an absence due to food poisoning?

Explain the need for extra care regarding personal hygiene controls

Which of the following statements is correct?
a) Disposable gloves are an acceptable alternative to handwashing
b) Hands must be washed before putting on disposable gloves
c) Disposable gloves do not need to be changed throughout the day
d) The same disposable gloves can be worn for handling raw and cooked meat

C. Hands must be washed before putting on disposable gloves

Which of the following is a personal hygiene habit that is most likely to contaminate food?
a) Sneezing or coughing into the shoulder
b) Preparing raw food and ready-to-eat food using the same knife
c) Storing food at room temperature
d) Sneezing or coughing near food

A. Sneezing or coughing near food

Which wall surfaces would be considered most suitable for use in a high-risk food room?

Glazed tiles

What are recommended properties for floor surfaces in a high-risk food room?

Joint-less, hard wearing, anti-slip and easy to clean.

Outside bins for food waste/rubbish should be?

Easy to clean with tight-fitting lids, hard wearing and of suitable size.

What is the main reason for linear workflow?

To reduce the risk of cross-contamination.

What is "disinfection?"

The reduction of micro-organisms to a safe level.

Which hazard is most likely to occur because of poor cleaning?

Contamination of food by micro-organisms.

Which of the following statements is true?
a) Harmful viruses can multiply on a poorly cleaned work surface
b) Cleaning materials should only be available in the morning
c) Floors of a food room should be disinfected at least daily
d) Sterilization is not necessary for work surfaces in food businesses

D. Sterilization is not necessary for work surfaces in food businesses.

Which of the following is the main responsibility of a supervisor regarding pest management?
a) To ensure staff report signs of pest infestation
b) To train food handlers to poison pests
c) To be able to maintain electric fly killers
d) To train food handlers to inspect rodent traps

A. To ensure staff report signs of pest infestation.

Which of the following are most important in reducing the risk of fly infestations in food premises?
a) Fly screens, covered waste receptacles and high standards of cleanliness
b) fly screens, covered waste receptacles and colour-coded food/rubbish bins
c) Protective clothing, fly screens and high standards of cleanliness
d) Fly screens, covered waste receptacles and tiled walls.

A. Fly screens, covered waste receptacles and high standards of cleanliness.

Which one of the following is included in the seven principles of HACCP?

a) Provide effective cleaning schedules
b) Provide staff with suitable protective clothing
c) Conduct a hazard analysis
d) Increase bacteriological testing

Conduct a hazard analysis.

What is the best way to stop rodents getting into a food premises?

Proofing, maintenance of drains & maintenance of buildings.

Which one of the following is a control measure?

a) Monitoring the effectiveness of cleaning
b) Disposing of the food if it smells off
c) Minimizing time at room temperature
d) Checking the temperature of food twice per day

C. Minimizing time at room temperature.

Monitoring records can be used to:

a) maintain the quality of the food
b) identify hazards
c) support due-diligence
d) set critical limits

C. Support due-diligence.

Which of the following statements is true?

a) Corrective action is not always needed when a critical limit is exceeded
b) Corrective action always involves disposing the food involved
c) Corrective action involves dealing with affected products and regaining process control
d) Corrective action is only concerned with bringing the process back under control

C. Corrective action involves dealing with affected products and regaining process control.

What is the best way of ensuring that cleaning and disinfection are carried out satisfactorily?

Using an effective cleaning schedule.

SAFETY SIGNS

Define safety signs?

Signs are warning of hazard; temporarily or permanently affixed or placed at locations where hazards exists.

What is the purpose of safety signs?

2. They keep us safe.
3. They save us time.
4. They keep others safe.
5. They keep us out of trouble.
6. They help the society find order.

7. **What is LOTO?**

Lock Out Tag Out. To lock out specific breakers are used for the maintenance of all equipment.

What are the types of safety signs?

8. Mandatory signs
9. Prohibitive signs
10. Warning signs
11. Safe Condition signs
12. Fire Equipment signs

Explain Mandatory signs.

They tell you what you **MUST** do. Instruct people to take a specific action. They are primarily used for P.P.Es instructions, e.g. 'Eye protection must be worn'. They are circular with a solid blue background and a white pictogram.

Explain Prohibitive signs.

They tell you what you **MUST NOT** do. They are directed at stopping dangerous human behavior, e.g. 'No parking'. They are circular with a black pictogram on a white background with a red border and red diagonal cross bar.

Explain Warning signs.

They tell you to be careful of a particular hazard, e.g. 'Forklift trucks operating in the area'. They are triangular signs with a black pictogram on a yellow background with a black border.

Explain Safe Condition signs.

They give information about first aid, fire escape or safe conditions. These signs identify safe behavior or places of safety, e.g. 'Assembly Point'. They are rectangular or square signs with a white pictogram on a green background.

Explain Fire Equipment signs.

They give you information about fire equipment. They identify particular items of fire equipment, e.g. 'Fire Extinguisher'. They are rectangular or square with a white symbol or pictogram on a red background.

What is meant by Barricade, Signals & Tags?

Barricade means an obstruction to deter the passage of persons or vehicles.

Signals are moving signs, provided by workers, such as flagmen, or by devices, such as flashing lights, to warn of possible or existing hazards.

Tags are temporary signs, usually attached to a piece of equipment or part of a structure, to warn of existing or immediate hazards.

What is safety tag?

Safety tag can be defined as a surface made of card board or paper board on which English/local language letters are written for warning and/or safety instructions to employees.

What is the importance of safety signs?

Safety Signs and Signals are one of the main means of communicating health and safety information.

This includes the use of illuminated signs, hand and acoustic signals (e.g. fire alarms), spoken communication and the marking of pipe work containing dangerous substances.

Traditional signboards, such as prohibition and warning signs, signs for fire exits, Fire Action Plan notices (fire drills) and fire-fighting equipment are also considered to be Safety Signs.

In view of their importance, it is critical that all Safety Signs and Signals can be easily understood.

What is the purpose of Notices, Posters and Films?

They are used to draw attention to hazards and risks or safe practices and measures, need to be 'eye catching' and relevant.

WELDING SAFETY

What is welding?

The process of joining of metals either by electrical or by gas is called welding.

What are types of welding hazards?

The types of welding hazards are:
- Radiation exposure
- Electric shock
- Fires and explosions
- Toxic Fumes and gases
- Loud noise etc.

During arc welding, what kind of electric shock risk is to the operator of the welding equipment?

Two kinds of electric shock can be experienced by the operator:
1. Primary voltage shock
2. Secondary voltage shock

Explain Primary voltage shock and Secondary voltage shock while performing arc welding.

Primary voltage shock: Primary voltage shock involves 230 or 460 volts and is caused by touching both the lead inside the welding equipment and the welding equipment case or other grounded metal while the equipment is powered ON.

Secondary voltage shock: Secondary voltage shock involves 60 to 100 watts and is caused by touching a part of the electrode circuit and the side of the welding circuit.

Name Eight Hazards associated with Manual Metal Arc Welding - (Electrical Welding)?

- Electric Shock.
- Burns.
- Ultra-Violet Radiation.
- Fire.
- Fumes.
- Arc - Eye.
- Slag Chipping in Eyes.
- Chemical Cleaning of Weld.
- Trailing Cables.

What are the control measures to reduce risk of electric shock during welding?

Do the following to avoid electric shock:
- Keep dry and wear dry gloves.
- Stand or lie on plywood, rubber mats or other insulation.
- Do not rest any part of the body on the work piece.
- Keep electrodes and electrode holders in good condition.
- Do not touch electrodes or metal parts with either the skin or wet clothing.

What are the control measures to reduce risk fire and explosion during welding?

Do the following to protect from fire and explosions:
- Always know where the fire exits and fire extinguishers are located.
- If welding within 35 feet of a combustible object, utilize a fire watcher, who can watch for landing sparks.
- The welding process can produce extreme heat; however, fire hazards are not caused by the heat but by the effect of the heat on the work piece, such as sparks and molten metal.
- Keep the work area and all surrounding areas free of combustible items.
- Be cautious when working in dusty areas where sparks and dust particles can easily oxidize without warning, which can result in a flash fire or an explosion.

What are the health effects of fumes and gases produced during welding process?

Fumes contain particles from base metal and base metal coating. Effects from fumes are normally temporary. Symptoms caused by short-term exposure to fumes can include burning eyes, burning skin, dizziness, nausea, and fever. Long-term exposure to fumes can cause siderosis (which are iron deposits in the lungs) and can affect pulmonary function.

Zinc fumes can cause metal fume fever, which is a temporary illness similar to the flu.

Cadmium fumes can cause symptoms similar to metal fume fever; however, it can be fatal, even under brief exposure.

When shielding gases are released into the air, they can cause dizziness, unconsciousness, and even death if clean oxygen is withheld for a long enough period.

UV radiation forms gases when it hits the air, which can cause headaches, chest pains, eye irritation and itchiness in the nose and throat.

What are the control measures for fumes and gases produced during welding process?

Do the following to protect from fume and gas exposure:
- Ensure adequate ventilation in the work area.
- Wear appropriate personal protective equipment, such as a respirator.
- Read material safety data sheets before beginning work to learn what fumes can be potentially released.
- Familiarize yourself with the metals that are being used to determine if a paint or coating can cause toxic fumes or gases.
- If symptoms of dizziness, headache, or nausea occur, turn off the welding equipment, notify supervisors and co-workers, and get fresh air immediately.

What are the control measures for welding in a confined space?

Do the following to protect yourself when working in confined spaces:
- Make sure your body is insulated from the work piece and ground.
- Wear dry gloves.
- Use only a well-insulated electrode holder.
- Verify that there is sufficient ventilation.
- Always make sure there is a trained person outside the confined space at all times to disconnect power and pull the welder out if a dangerous situation occurs.

What are the control measures for loud noise created during welding process?

Loud noise can cause temporary or permanent hearing loss. Do the following to protect against noise:
- Reduce the sound level when possible.
- Wear ear muffs or ear plugs.

What are the first aid procedures for heat exhaustion due to welding process?

First of all recognize the symptoms like:
- Extreme perspiration
- Pale, clammy skin
- Rapid, weak pulse
- Rapid shallow breathing

If confirmed then:
- Immediately move the victim to a cool place.
- Lay victim flat and elevate the feet slightly.
- Remove as much of the victim's clothing as possible.
- Sponge the skin with cool water.

What should be lockout / tagout policy for defective welding equipment?

- Obtain permission from a supervisor before you plan to lockout a piece of equipment.
- Shut off the equipment.
- Place the locks on the switches and valves.
- Try to start the equipment or open the valves.
- Begin working.
- When the work is completed, verify that all employees are cleared of the equipment before removing the locks and tags.
- Write a brief message on the tag, if necessary.
- Write your name and the date.
- Attach the tag in a visible location.

The two hoses on an oxygen-acetylene welding/cutting set are colored differently. Give the two colors and which is which?

Blue: Oxygen.
Red: Acetylene.

When should screens be arranged around a welding job?

When there is a danger to others working nearby.

Why does a person using an electrical welding process wear special eye protection?

To protect the eyes from Ultra-Violet Rays.

What type of ventilation is suitable for dealing with fumes, which arise from point sources such as grinding or welding?

Local exhaust ventilation.

MECHANICAL HAZARDS

What are the causes of machine accidents?

- Reaching in to "clear" equipment
- Not using Lockout/Tagout
- Unauthorized persons doing maintenance or using the machines
- Missing or loose machine guards

Where Mechanical Hazards occur on a machine?

- Point of operation
- All parts of the machine which move, such as:
    - Flywheels, pulleys, belts, couplings, chains, cranks, gears, etc.
    - Feed mechanisms and auxiliary parts of the machine
- In-running nip points

All parts of the machine which move while the machine is working can cause mechanical hazards. These can include reciprocating, rotating, and transverse moving parts, as well as feed mechanisms and auxiliary parts of the machine.

What is Point of Operation?

That point where work is performed on the material such as cutting, shaping, boring or forming of stock and which must be guarded.

How in-running nip point can cause hazards to a machine user?

In-running nip point hazards are caused by the rotating parts on machinery. There are three main types of in-running nips.

1. Parts can rotate in opposite directions while their axes are parallel to each other. These parts may be in contact (producing a nip point) or in close proximity to each other (where the stock fed between the rolls produces the nip points). This danger is common on machinery with intermeshing gears and rotating cylinders.
2. Another type of nip point is created between rotating and tangentially moving parts; for example, a chain and a sprocket, a rack and pinion, or the point of contact between a power transmission belt and its pulley.
3. Nip points can also occur between rotating and fixed parts which create a shearing, crushing, or abrading action; for example, spoked hand wheels or flywheels, screw conveyors, or the periphery of an abrasive wheel and an incorrectly adjusted work rest.

Name drive mechanisms which you would associate with in-running nips?

- Belt
- Chains
- Gear drives
- Conveyor systems
- Revolving shafts, couplings, spindles, mandrels, bars and flywheels
- In-running nips between pairs of rotating parts
- In-running nips of the belt and pulley type
- Projections on revolving parts
- Discontinuous revolving parts
- Revolving beaters, spiked cylinders and revolving drums
- Revolving cutting tools
- Reciprocating needles

What are Requirements for Safeguards?

- Prevent contact - prevent worker's body or clothing from contacting hazardous moving parts
- Secure - firmly secured to machine and not easily removed
- Protect from falling objects - ensure that no objects can fall into moving parts
- Create no new hazards - must not have shear points, jagged edges or unfinished surfaces
- Create no interference - must not prevent worker from performing the job quickly and comfortably
- Allow safe lubrication - if possible, be able to lubricate the machine without removing the safeguards

In hierarchy, methods of machine safeguarding are?

Guards
- Fixed
- Interlocked
- Adjustable
- Self-adjusting

Devices
- Presence sensing
- Pullback
- Restraint
- Safety controls (tripwire cable, two-hand control)
- Gates

Location/distance

Feeding and ejection methods
- Automatic and/or semi-automatic feed and ejection
- Robots

Miscellaneous aids
- Awareness barriers
- Protective shields
- Hand-feeding tools

List eight areas where you might see "entanglement"?

- Drill chucks
- Couplings
- Screw drives
- Smooth rotating shafts
- Conveyor systems
- Revolving shafts, couplings, spindles, mandrels, bars and flywheels
- In-running nips between pairs of rotating parts
- In-running nips of the belt and pulley type
- Projections on revolving parts
- Discontinuous revolving parts
- Revolving beaters, spiked cylinders and revolving drums
- Revolving cutting tools
- Reciprocating needles

When may it be required to remove or override a guard? Give four instances?

May be required during:
- Maintenance operations
- Lubrication
- Tool setting
- Gauging
- Removing jams

List hazards that can arise from the use of abrasive wheels?

- Improper selection of wheel
- Improper mounting
- Over speed
- Inadequate guarding
- Rotating parts
- Flying particles
- Source of ignition
- Imbalance
- Dust
- Noise

What are trip mechanisms / interlocks?

Devices that:
- Automatically cut the power from the machine
- Operate an emergency brake to stop the machine, if the guard is opened while the machine is operating.

An interlocked guard may use electrical, mechanical, hydraulic, or pneumatic power or any combination of these. Interlocks should not prevent "inching" by remote control, if required. Replacing the guard should not automatically restart the machine.

What are Machine Safety Responsibilities for different category of employees?

Management
- Ensure all machinery is properly guarded.

Supervisors
- Train employees on specific guard rules in their areas.
- Ensure machine guards remain in place and are functional.
- Immediately correct machine guard deficiencies.

Employees
- Do not remove guards unless machine is locked and tagged.
- Report machine guard problems to supervisors immediately.
- Do not operate equipment unless guards are in place.

Outside of knifes, list six cutting edges associated with work equipment?

- Circular saw blades
- Meat slicers
- Rough surfaces
- Grinding wheels
- Sanding belts
- Guillotines
- Shredding machines.

In the context of work equipment what is a trap?

A trap is where a part of the body can get caught in part of the mechanism and cannot be removed without injury.

List means of power transmission?

- A simple shaft or direct drive
- Power Take Off (PTO)
- Speed changing mechanism
- Gears
- Belts and pulleys
- Chains and sprockets.

MANUAL HANDLING

What is Ergonomics?

The study of work; or
The discipline that matches the job to the worker; or
The study of relationship between the worker, the work that they are doing, and the environment in which they are doing it.

What is Upper Limb Disorders (ULDs)?

Upper Limb Disorders (ULDs) are:
- Aches, pains, tension and disorders involving any part of the arm from fingers to shoulder, or the neck,
- Include problems with the soft tissues muscles, tendons and ligaments, along with the circulatory and nerve supply to the limb; and
- Are often caused or made worse by work.

What causes an ULD?

- Repetitive work.
- Uncomfortable working postures.
- Sustained or excessive force.
- Carrying out a task for a long period of time.
- Poor working environment and organization (e.g. temperature, lighting and work pressure, job demands, work breaks or lack of them).
- Individual differences and susceptibility (some workers are more affected by certain risks).

MSDs stands for?

Musculoskeletal Disorders

What is Tendon?

A tendon (or sinew) is a tough band of fibrous connective tissue that usually connects muscle to bone and is capable of withstanding tension.

What is Ligament?

A short band of tough, flexible fibrous connective tissue which connects two bones or cartilages or holds together a joint.

What are key risk factors for ULDs?

Key risk factors can be thought of as task, individual worker, or environment related.

What does the acronym T.I.L.E. stand for?

Task, Individual, Load & Environment.

What risk factors to consider when doing risk assessment for ULDs using T.I.L.E.

Task & Individual
- Movement frequency; arms, wrists, fingers, neck
- Duration of work / rest break patterns
- Posture (full body and arms)
- Workstation set-up / design
- Individual differences / vulnerable people

Forces being applied
- Gripping, pushing, twisting, pinching etc.

Environmental factors
- Physical environment
- Psychosocial factors

List risks from manual handling?

- Risk of accidental injury
- Risk of overexertion
- Risk of cumulative damage.

Name the part of the spine that is most involved in manual handling?

Lumbar spine.

Give types of injuries that can be caused by Incorrect Methods of Manual Lifting?

- Hernia.
- Back-strain.
- Sprained Ligaments.
- Strained Muscles.

Why practice correct handling. Give reasons?

- The muscles best suited for the job are used.

- Because it reduces the strain.
- It protects against sudden injury.

What is the correct way to lift?

Bend the knees, keep back straight, and chin in, use strong thigh muscles.

When handling a load name four points to observe before lifting?

- Good grip available.
- Check weight.
- Look for sharp edges.
- Watch for traps.

What is most important with a large load even if light?

It should not obscure the vision.

Before moving a load what two general things should you do?

1. Size up the load.
2. Remove possible hazards.

When handling heavy drums, cylinders etc. How do you use the body?

Use it as a counter balance to reduce muscular effort.

Give reasons why you should bend your knees to lift?

- So that leg muscles do the lifting
- A good lifting posture can be adopted
- The load can be reached without arching the spine.

List safer handling principles?

- Assess the area and the load
- Adopt a broad stable base
- Keep the back straight
- Bend the knees
- Get a firm grip
- Keep the load close to the body
- Keep arms in line with the trunk
- Turn the feet in the direction of movement.

Other than the weight of the load, give six other factors that should be considered when handling a load?

1. Size or shape of the load
2. Carrying distance
3. Lift level
4. Environment factors
5. Degree of twisting involved
6. Work rate

What is the recommended height to which one person should manually lift an object, and what should they do if they need to put it higher?

Chest Height - If the object needs to be placed higher, then unless the object is very light two people should do the task.

In relation to the manual handling of a load there are nine essential points in respect of the characterizing of the load that may present a risk particularly of back injury. Can you name them?

1. Load too heavy.
2. Load too large.
3. Unwieldy Load.
4. Load difficult to grasp.
5. Unstable Load.
6. Load contents likely to shift.
7. Load has to be held at distance from trunk of body.
8. Load requires bending or twisting of trunk.
9. Contours of load creating further hazard in event of collision.

List few Ergonomic guidelines for ULDs.

Work station layout
- Achieve better working heights
- Reduce reach distances
- Use of deflectors on conveyors

Good lighting
Suitable tools for tasks
- Tools with sufficient power / sharpness / accuracy

Production line speed
- Reduce speed
- Increase number of staff on the production line
- Improve preparation
- Deal with stopping the line
- Control / limit the forces being applied / weights being handled
- Deal with reluctance to stop lines

What do the acronyms 'WRULD' and 'RSI' stand for?

- Work Related Upper Limb Disorder
- Repetitive Strain Injury

What part of the body is affected by Carpal Tunnel Syndrome?

The hand.

What is "Anthropometrics"?

It is the branch of ergonomics that deals with the physical size and shape of people.

There are four factors which, when combined, can give rise to RSI. Name them?

1. Force
2. High repetition
3. Awkward posture
4. Insufficient rest

Give four possible reactions of an individual to stress?

1. Physical reaction
2. Psychological reaction
3. Emotional reaction
5. Behavioral reaction

For standing work, what is the recommended work surface height for men involved in precision work?

109cm - 110cm

Give four environmental factors which should be considered in an ergonomic assessment?

1. Noise
2. Humidity
3. Vibration
4. Light
5. Temperature
6. Ventilation

In relation to VDUs, what is the optimum lighting level that should be maintained at the workstation?

300 to 500 lux

Name six physical characteristics of the individual that should be considered in ergonomics?

1. Body size
2. Body shape
3. Fitness
4. Strength
5. Posture
6. The senses
7. Stresses and strains on muscles, joints nerves

OFF-SHORE SAFETY

List few hazards on an off-shore rig.

1. Explosion.
2. Toxic gas.
3. Exposure to drowning.
4. Physical risks & accidents.
5. Diving risks.
6. Aviation risks.
7. Weather conditions.

What methods can be used to arrive on an off-shore rig?

- Helicopter transportation.
- Boat transportation.
- Swing ropes.
- Personnel baskets.

What are simultaneous operations?

Simultaneous Operations (SimOps) is defined as performing two or more of the following operations concurrently:
- Production Operations
- Rig Operations
- Construction Operations (Includes Electrical and Instrumentation I&E)
- Anchoring of Vessels
- Derrick Barge Operations
- Heavy Lifts by Stationary Cranes over Pressurized Equipment
- Diving Operations

Who is person in charge (PIC)?

A PIC shall be designated on the Simultaneous Operations Plan. The PIC is the liaison between the various operations involved. The PIC is in charge of all simultaneous operations procedures and is the:
- Drill Site Managers (DSM) or Well Site Managers (WSM) on all rig operations.
- Production Representative (OS, FC, etc.) on all non-rig operations.
- Other by Management designation.

MODU & MIDU stands for?

- MODU stand for Mobile Offshore Drilling Unit.
- MIDU stands for Mobile Inland Drilling Unit.

In a man overboard situation, what four actions should you take?

1. Raise the alarm by shouting man overboard
2. Immediately throw the lifebuoy, together with its smoke float and light.
3. Inform the Officer on Watch so that he can mark the position
4. Act as a lookout, and point to the person continually.

Apart from failure to locate the person give four reasons for life being lost in a man overboard situation?

1. Drowning.
2. Loss of consciousness due to Hypothermia.
3. Cold Shock.
4. Injury in the rescue.

When is it essential to wear life jackets after cast off?

At all times when completing hazardous deck work.

While standing on the bridge of a ship facing the stern, what do you call the deck at the stern in nautical terms?

Poop Deck.

What do you call the deck that the lifeboats are on?

The Boat Deck.

What do you call the deck that has the hatch covers on it?

The Well Deck.

While standing on the bridge of a ship facing the bow, what color navigation lights would you find on your right-hand side?

Green.

While standing on the bridge of a ship facing the bow, what color navigation lights would you find on your left-hand side?

Red.

Where on a boat would you expect to find the Jackstaff?

The Bow.

Where on a boat would you expect to find the Ensign staff?

The Stern.

What is the principal danger if boat approaches some body in the water in a man overboard situation apart from fouling of the propeller by ropes and lines being used in the rescue?

The boat may drift down on top of the person.

Give four pieces of personal protective equipment which should be issued to all crew members?

1. Life jackets
2. Buoyancy Aids
3. Protective clothing suitable for the Industry
4. Suitable footwear.

What is essential to have fitted to close fitting inflatable life jackets?

An electronic homing device.

What is the function of the line painted on the side of a ship?

To indicate the maximum load.

What is the name of the line painted on the side of a ship?

The Plimsoll Line

While standing on the bridge of a ship facing the bow, what do you call the side of the ship on your right-hand side in nautical terms?

Starboard Side.

While standing on the bridge of a ship facing the bow, what do you call the side of the ship on your left-hand side in nautical terms?

Port Side.

While standing on the bridge of a ship facing the bow, what do you call the deck at the bow in nautical terms?

Forecastle Deck.

What are the three European Standards of Lifejacket?

They are 100 Newtons, 150 Newtons & 275 Newtons.

What is the equivalent flotation support for a 'Newton'?

10 Newtons is the equivalent of 1 Kg of flotation support.

What is a buoyancy aid?

A buoyancy aid will simply help a conscious person to keep afloat.

What is a Racon Beacon?

It is a device that, on receiving radar signals, transmits coded signals in response to help navigators determine their position.

Lifejackets and safety harnesses are essential and should be provided for everyone on board. What other items are essential, and what is essential about lifejackets, and what else is essential to know?

- Ensure sets of warm and protective clothing are available including sunglasses
- They could ensure your survival, but only if worn
- Everyone must know what to do in a man overboard situation - It could be YOU.

Being able to call help is important at sea in case of emergency. List three methods that you can use?

- A VHF radio, which can be used to call the coast guard or another boat.
- Carry a portable foghorn
- The whistle fitted to your lifejacket to attract attention
- Mobile phone. (Cannot be depended on as coverage is problematic).

Give eight instances that may cause a boat to get into difficulties?

1. Very bad weather e.g. storm conditions.
2. Engine failure.
3. Fire on Board.
4. Malfunction of the rudder or steering equipment.
5. Malfunction of Navigational equipment.
6. Collision with rocks or other object
7. Malfunction of the radio or radar equipment.
8. Lack of proper training of the crew.

Give eight life saving devices or equipment which should be carried on a fishing boat?

1. Life Buoys.
2. Life Jackets
3. Life Boats.
4. Life Rafts.
5. Life lines and harness
6. Flares.
7. Communication Equipment.
8. Personal Protective Equipment.

Give eight ways of avoiding accidents at sea?

1. Correct lighting, particularly in hours of darkness.
2. Fog warning in poor visibility conditions.
3. Proper monitoring of radio gale warnings.
4. Regular maintenance of engine and equipment.
5. Correct balancing of cargo.
6. Prevention of overloading.
7. Proper watch keeping and lookout.
8. Correct covering of hatches.
9. Reduce speed when necessary.
10. Regular emergency drills for crews.

TRANSPORT SAFETY

Before starting to move a vehicle what should be done?

Look all round it.

Why should a forklift truck have its forks at the lowest point when loaded?

To lower the center of gravity and give the driver a better view.

Why should a forklift truck have its forks at the lowest point when unloaded?

It is the safest position.

When carrying high loads, in which direction would you, drive a forklift truck?

In reverse.

Do you consider forklift truck driving a skilled job?

Yes.

How often should maintenance be done on trucks?

Daily.

How can traffic be controlled in a factory yard?

Use signs and marking similar to those used on the roads.

What is essential about painted signs on roadways?

They should be clearly visible and well maintained.

What is the legal age to drive a tractor on a farm?

14 years.

Name four Safety Factors to be exercised when using mobile equipment within a works or site?

1. Watch out for overhead obstruction.
2. Be extra careful at corners.
3. Avoid uneven or soft ground.
4. Keep the speed down.
5. Secure loaded materials properly.

Give four points of care when loading a hand truck?

- Not too high.
- Properly stacked.
- Properly balanced.
- Secure.

Give the four main points to consider when guiding a driver in his lorry?

- Have a clear view.
- Stand in full view.
- Keep a keen lookout.
- Give clear signals.

At what length is it necessary to display a "Long Vehicle" sign?

13 meters or 40 feet.

What is the recommended minimum safe distance between two forklifts travelling in the same direction?

Three truck lengths.

What two essential considerations must be taken into account in deciding the dimensions of routes used for safe pedestrian and / or goods traffic?

1. The number of potential users.
2. Type of undertaking involved.

What two specific safety considerations are required in the equipping of escalators and travellators?

1. Any necessary safety devices.
2. Easily identifiable and accessible shutdown devices.

Give eight instances that may cause a boat to get into difficulties?

1. Very bad weather e.g. storm conditions.
2. Engine failure.
3. Fire on Board.
4. Malfunction of the rudder or steering equipment.
5. Malfunction of Navigational equipment.
6. Collision with rocks or other object
7. Malfunction of the radio or radar equipment.
8. Lack of proper training of the crew.

Give eight life saving devices or equipment which should be carried on a fishing boat?

1. Life Buoys.
2. Life Jackets
3. Life Boats.
4. Life Rafts.
5. Life lines and harness
6. Flares.
7. Communication Equipment.
8. Personal Protective Equipment.

Give eight ways of avoiding accidents at sea?

1. Correct lighting, particularly in hours of darkness.
2. Fog warning in poor visibility conditions.
3. Proper monitoring of radio gale warnings.
4. Regular maintenance of engine and equipment.
5. Correct balancing of cargo.
6. Prevention of overloading.
7. Proper watch keeping and lookout.
8. Correct covering of hatches.
9. Reduce speed when necessary.
10. Regular emergency drills for crews.

TRANSPORT SAFETY

Before starting to move a vehicle what should be done?

Look all round it.

Why should a forklift truck have its forks at the lowest point when loaded?

To lower the center of gravity and give the driver a better view.

Why should a forklift truck have its forks at the lowest point when unloaded?

It is the safest position.

When carrying high loads, in which direction would you, drive a forklift truck?

In reverse.

Do you consider forklift truck driving a skilled job?

Yes.

How often should maintenance be done on trucks?

Daily.

How can traffic be controlled in a factory yard?

Use signs and marking similar to those used on the roads.

What is essential about painted signs on roadways?

They should be clearly visible and well maintained.

What is the legal age to drive a tractor on a farm?

14 years.

Name four Safety Factors to be exercised when using mobile equipment within a works or site?

1. Watch out for overhead obstruction.
2. Be extra careful at corners.
3. Avoid uneven or soft ground.
4. Keep the speed down.
5. Secure loaded materials properly.

Give four points of care when loading a hand truck?

- Not too high.
- Properly stacked.
- Properly balanced.
- Secure.

Give the four main points to consider when guiding a driver in his lorry?

- Have a clear view.
- Stand in full view.
- Keep a keen lookout.
- Give clear signals.

At what length is it necessary to display a "Long Vehicle" sign?

13 meters or 40 feet.

What is the recommended minimum safe distance between two forklifts travelling in the same direction?

Three truck lengths.

What two essential considerations must be taken into account in deciding the dimensions of routes used for safe pedestrian and / or goods traffic?

1. The number of potential users.
2. Type of undertaking involved.

What two specific safety considerations are required in the equipping of escalators and travellators?

1. Any necessary safety devices.
2. Easily identifiable and accessible shutdown devices.

Where are loading bays over a certain length required to have Exit Points located?

At each end.

What two essential safety requirements are necessary where mechanical doors and gates are used for building entry?

1. Emergency shut down devices must be fitted.
2. They must be capable of manual operation, unless they open automatically on power failure.

What is a 'rider-operated lift truck'?

A 'rider-operated lift truck' means any truck capable of carrying an operator, including trucks controlled from both seated and stand-on positions, which may be fixed or foldaway.

Should a non-integrated working platform be CE marked, explain your answer?

NO. As the occasional use of non-integrated working platforms is only allowed in some EU member states, there is no free movement of these platforms allowed throughout the EU, and, as such, they must not be CE marked.

List four precautions which should be taken to minimize risk from driving at work?

- Plan work to minimize driving requirements
- Ensure that the vehicle is maintained in accordance with the manufacturer's instructions, including specific winter and summer precautions
- Take sensible breaks and seek to avoid overlong days of work and driving
- Follow the personal safety precautions outlined in the Lone Worker arrangements
- Report the development of any health problem which may limit or prevent driving (such as epilepsy)

List four activities that should be considered when carrying out risk assessments for transport?

Activities may include:
- Arrival and departure;
- Travel within the workplace;
- Loading, unloading and securing loads;
- Sheeting;
- Coupling; and shunting
- Vehicle maintenance work.

What is a TREMCARD, where would you expect to find it, and what information would it give you?

It is a "Transport Emergency Card". It is carried by vehicles carrying hazardous materials.
It would tell you,
- The name of the material being carried.
- A description of its appearance and properties.
- Its hazards and precautions against these hazards.
- The action necessary in the event of fire or spillage.

What is the minimum level of training required for lift truck operators? Give three points?

- Basic training must be given on all the types of lift truck that operators will or could be required to use
- Training in all attachments that operators will or could be required to use in their work.
- Note should be taken of Code of Practice on Rider-operated lift trucks
- In the case of novice drivers a 5 day training course should be considered.

What is the difference between an integrated working platform and a non-integrated working platform for forklifts?

An integrated working platform is an attachment on a forklift:-
- With controls that are linked to and isolate the truck controls.
- So that only the person in the platform can control the lift height of the platform.
- So that only the person in the platform can control the truck movements.

A non-integrated working platform is an attachment for use in conjunction with a forklift truck.
- That elevates people, but they have no controls in the platform.
- All truck and working platform movements are controlled by the truck operator.
- The use of this type of platform is only permitted in exceptional circumstances.

What safe work practices should be considered before driving an All-Terrain Vehicle (ATV). Give three?

The following safe practices should be considered:-
- Provide all drivers with adequate training. There is a legal requirement for employers and the self-employed to ensure training for work equipment such as ATVs.

- Operators must take note of manufacturer's instructions particularly those relating to driving on slopes and rough terrain.
- Plan the use of ATVs carefully and take particular note of variations in ground conditions and gradient.
- Remember increasing speed increases vehicle instability and the risk of overturning.
- Wear head protection, which protects the head and neck. Protective helmets which meet BS 6658:1985 are suitable.

Tractors are potentially lethal and accidents involving tractors account for a very high proportion of all farm accidents each year. What six steps can be taken on farms to prevent accidents involving tractors?

1. Ensure that the tractor is maintained in good working condition
2. Ensure that a cab or safety frame is fitted
3. Ensure that all controls are in good working order and clearly marked
4. Ensure that brakes are checked regularly and are always in sound working condition
5. Ensure that all relevant guards are in place and that PTO and Hydraulics are functioning correctly
6. Ensure that mirrors, lights and wipers are in working order at all times
7. Ensure that the tractor is always parked safely

In most years up to half the fatal workplace accidents involve vehicles at the place of work. In addition, many more people are seriously injured. List six common accidents related to vehicles?

- Being struck or run over by a vehicle or its trailer
- Falling from vehicles
- People being struck or suffocated by a load
- Vehicles overturning
- Vehicles running out of control
- Vehicles touching power lines
- Vehicles being driven by untrained drivers

Diesel engine exhaust emissions (commonly known as 'diesel fumes') are a mixture of gases, vapors, liquid aerosols and substances made up of particles. They contain the products of combustion. List six components of diesel engine exhaust emissions?

- Carbon (soot).
- Nitrogen.
- Water.
- Carbon monoxide.
- Aldehydes.
- Nitrogen dioxide.
- Sulphur dioxide.
- Polycyclic aromatic hydrocarbons.

List six effects diesel and diesel fumes can have on your health?

- Irritation of the eyes or respiratory tract
- Coughing
- Chestiness
- Breathlessness
- Dermatitis
- Lung cancer

Workplace transport means any vehicle that is used in a work setting, list six?

- Forklift trucks
- Compact dumpers
- Tractors
- Mobile cranes
- Cars
- Vans
- Large goods vehicles

Drivers should never leave their vehicle without ensuring that the vehicle and its trailer are in what state. List six?

- Securely braked
- Engine is stopped
- The starter key removed
- Mounted equipment lowered to the ground
- Trailer chocked
- Safely parked

Vehicles at the workplace must be safe and suitable for work for which they are being used. List eight aspects that may have to be taken into account?

1. Are vehicles purchased or leased with all the recommended safety features? (This is particularly important when second-hand vehicles are purchased or leased).
2. Do they have suitable and effective service and parking brakes?
3. Are they provided with horns, lights, reflectors,
4. Reversing lights, alarms and other safety features as necessary?
5. Do they have seats and, where necessary, seat belts that are safe and allow for driver comfort?
6. Are there guards on dangerous parts of the vehicles, e.g. power take offs, chains drives, exposed exhaust pipes?

7. Do drivers need protection against bad weather conditions, or against an unpleasant working environment, e.g. against cold, dirt, dust, fumes and excessive noise and vibration?
8. Is there a safe means of access to and exit from the cabs and other parts that need to be reached?
9. Is there a need for driver protection against injury in the event of an overturn, and to prevent the driver being hit by falling objects?
10. Is there a necessity for closed circuit television (CCT) or sensors for reversing?
11. Is there a need for emergency stops outside the vehicle?

If you have a child or young person aged 14 or over and you have permitted them to drive a tractor or self-propelled machine on the farm, what eight steps should you take before you allow them to drive?

1. Ensure that they have attended a formal training course run by a competent training provider.
2. Ensure that they are closely supervised by a responsible adult.
3. Ensure that they have the ability to operate the controls with ease.
4. Ensure that all the controls are conveniently accessible for safe operation by the operator when seated in the driver's seat.
5. Ensure that the controls which operate the power take off (PTO) devices, hydraulic devices and engine cut-off are clearly marked to show the effect of their operation.
6. Ensure that the tractor is maintained so that it is safe for them to operate.
7. Ensure that the ground over which the tractor is driven is free from hazards such as steep slopes or excavations, river banks, lake or pond edges, deep ditches and similar areas.
8. Ensure that the young person is not accompanied by a friend, who would not have received training.

VENTILATION SAFETY

Ventilation is an example of which control measure?

Engineering Control

What is the reason for good ventilation?

To render harmless dust and fumes.

How should adequate ventilation be provided?

By circulation of fresh air.

What is a dust cloud?

Small particles of solid matter dispersed in air.

What is the best way of controlling harmful dusts?

Remove them at the source.

What is the reason for good ventilation?

To render harmless dust and fumes.

If a confined space has not been certified as safe, can a person enter it?

Yes, if they are wearing breathing apparatus.

Does a dust mask give protection against fumes?

No.

Name two types of respiratory protection?

- Dust Mask.
- Gas Mask (Cartridge) & Breathing Apparatus.

What type of ventilation is suitable for dealing with fumes, which arise from point sources such as grinding or welding?

Local exhaust ventilation.

What type of ventilation is suitable for dealing with low concentrations of low toxicity substances?

General ventilation

Why are right angle bends bad in ducting?

Eddy currents are caused and efficiency reduced.

Should ducting inlets be bigger than outlets?

Yes, inlets should be bigger than outlets.

Name two of the Authorities who have regulatory control over dust and fume emissions?

1. The Local Authority.
2. The Environmental Protection Agency.
3. The Health and Safety Authority.

Name two important points in relation to air filter operation?

- Cleaned regularly
- Efficiently maintained.

If work has to be done in an enclosed space, what two things should be done before entry?

- Ventilated.
- Tested.

If a room is being ventilated for fumes that are heavier than air, where should the inlets and outlets be placed?

The inlets are high and the outlets are low.

If a room is being ventilated for fumes that are lighter than air, where should the inlets and outlets be placed?

The inlets are low and the outlets are high.

What is the best system for heavier than air fumes?

Sucked through slots in floor & removed to safe place.

If fumes are flammable, what two things are necessary about the fan motor?

1. Suitable Electrical Classification.
2. Sited outside exhaust stream.

If lack of oxygen is suspected, what should be done?

Tests made and fresh air supplied.

The movement of air by a fan appears to reduce the temperature in a room. Does it reduce the room temperature, explain your answer?

No it does not reduce the room temperature, it passes the air over the body thus increasing the heat loss and reducing body temperature.

Give four factors on which the effects of dust on the respiratory system depend?

- The type of dust.
- The toxicity of the dust.
- Particle size distribution.
- Amount of dust entering lungs.
- State of health of the individual & his Tolerance.

Which unit of measure is normally used to measure the size of dust particles?

Micron, or Micrometer.

The danger of a dust to health depends very much on the size of the particles. Which of the following are the most dangerous and why? (a) 0.2 microns to 5.0 microns. (b) 200.0 microns to 500.0 microns. (c) 5.0 mm to 10 mm.

a) 0.2 microns to 5.0 microns. Larger particles are usually unable to penetrate the lung defenses.

What instrument is used to study dust clouds which is named after its inventor?

Tyndallometer

What is the difference between smoke and fumes?

Smoke - is a suspension of solid particles produced by incomplete combustion of organic material.
Fumes - are produced by sublimation or condensation of volatile solids, which may not be as a result of combustion.

What is the difference between a gas and a vapor?

Gas - is a substance that exists only in gaseous form at standard temperature and pressure.
Vapor - is the gaseous form of a substance normally found as a liquid at standard temperature and pressure.

With exhaust ventilation systems which is best, qualify your answer (a) large openings with slow moving air or (b) small openings with fast moving air?

(b) Because the greater the velocity the greater the quantities of dust etc. that are removed.

The types of Dust Extraction Equipment can be classified into four main areas based on the principal utilized. Name three of the four?

1. Centrifugal Separation.
2. Wet Scrubbing.
3. Electrostatic Precipitation.
4. Filtration.

In designing a local exhaust ventilating system there are five essential parts to consider. Name three of them?

1. The source of the dust.
2. The Hood.
3. The Ducting.
4. The air cleaning plant.
5. The Fan.

Name three types of test equipment which check ventilation performance?

- Smoke Tubes: these give a visual assessment of the capture of at a ventilation hood.
- Pressure Gauges, Manometers, or Pitot Tubes: measure pressure drops.
- Vane Anemometers: measure velocity of flow.

Name six of the general contributors to air pollution?

1. Smoke.
2. Sulphur Dioxide.
3. Particles.
4. Nitrogen Oxides.
5. Carbon Monoxide.
6. Lead.
7. Hydrocarbons.
8. Radioactivity.
9. Grits & Dusts.

TOOLS SAFETY

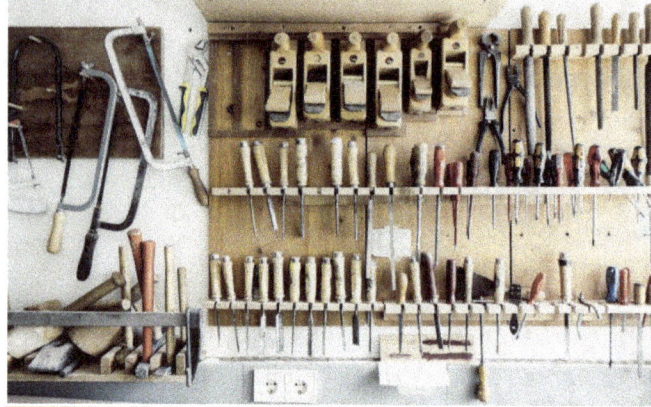

Why should a file not be struck with a hammer or other hard object?

The highly tempered metal is brittle and is most likely to shatter.

What must be done with tangs of files?

Handles must be fitted before using the file.

Mushroom heads on chisels may cause flying chips of metal. What should you do?

Grind them with a slight bevel towards the head to prevent mushrooming.

Give two faults that may develop in a hammer?

- Loose head.
- Split handle.
- Mushroomed head.

What should be done with defective tools?

They should not be used, and either repaired or rejected.

When using knives, should you cut towards the body or away from it?

Away from it.

Must all portable electric tools be earthed?

Yes, unless they are of the double insulated type.

What should be done with defective tools?

They should be rejected and returned.

What four precautions must be taken when using a spanner or key?

- Correct size.
- Good condition.
- Do not lengthen.
- No finger traps.

Give four hazards of cartridge operated tools?

1. Ricochets.
2. Rebounds.
3. Going through.
4. Noise.

The efficiency and safe working of grinders and grinderettes depend on what two conditions?

- The correct wheel for the job.
- The wheel properly mounted.

There are two types of cut off discs available, reinforced or unreinforced. Which should be used on portable hand held machines?

The Reinforced type.

Which of the following type of discs, aluminum oxide or silicon carbide, should be used for grinding masonry or cast iron?

Silicon Carbide.

Name the most likely machine in a metal working factory that you might expect to find guarded by infra-red light beams?

A Press Brake.

Name four safety features concerning portable electric grinding machines?

1. The machine should be double insulated.
2. The power cable should have a tough sheath and be connected to a proper plug incorporating an earth connection.
3. The machine should be well maintained and the earth connection tested.
4. The use of low power, center point tapped transformer is recommended.
5. The machine should not be lifted, lowered, or dragged by its power cable.

www.ingramcontent.com/pod-product-compliance
Lightning Source LLC
Chambersburg PA
CBHW060435220526
45465CB00008B/3154